Dearest Munda
With love & best wishes
[signature]
17 June 2011

LIZ BREWER'S
ULTIMATE GUIDE
to PARTY PLANNING
& ETIQUETTE

*"The Midas touch of
the Party World"*
DAME SHIRLEY BASSEY

*"The quintessential party creator
and guide to social behaviour
in the 21st Century"*
IVANA TRUMP

LIZ BREWER'S ULTIMATE GUIDE *to* PARTY PLANNING & ETIQUETTE

*Dedicated to my enchanting and talented
daughter Tallulah Rendall.*

Acknowledgements

To all those friends whose parties I have shared and without whom this book could not have been written.

Sincere thanks and acknowledgement, to those who allowed their photographs or illustrations to be used. Every reasonable attempt has been made to contact all photographers; we thank them for their contribution.

The extract from Party Cocktails by Ian Wisniewski is reproduced by kind permission of the publisher, Conran Octopus.

Front cover photographer: **Brendon O'Sullivan**
Back cover style director: **Mohieb Dahabieh**
Photographs from Dame Shirley Bassey's birthday
kindly contributed by **Edward Lloyd**

Cartoons and line-drawings: Liz Brewer
Editor: Liz Brewer

Printed in Britain by Dynasty Press Ltd

LIZ BREWER'S ULTIMATE GUIDE *to* PARTY PLANNING & ETIQUETTE

A PERSONAL EXPLANATION AND GUIDE
TO HELP ANSWER QUESTIONS MANY
PEOPLE ARE RELUCTANT TO ASK

Written and illustrated by

LIZ BREWER

DYNASTY PRESS

You have to have a dream
...and you have to make
that dream happen

LIZ BREWER

The Fame Game
BBC TV

contents

contents

Robert Newmark,
Tallulah Rendall and
Andrew Logan (the Lion)
celebrating Zandra Rhodes
70th birthday

9

In order to write my first book I created this Party tree. Each leaf was an important ingredient and each branch was a chapter. For the first time it is being shown in its original state.

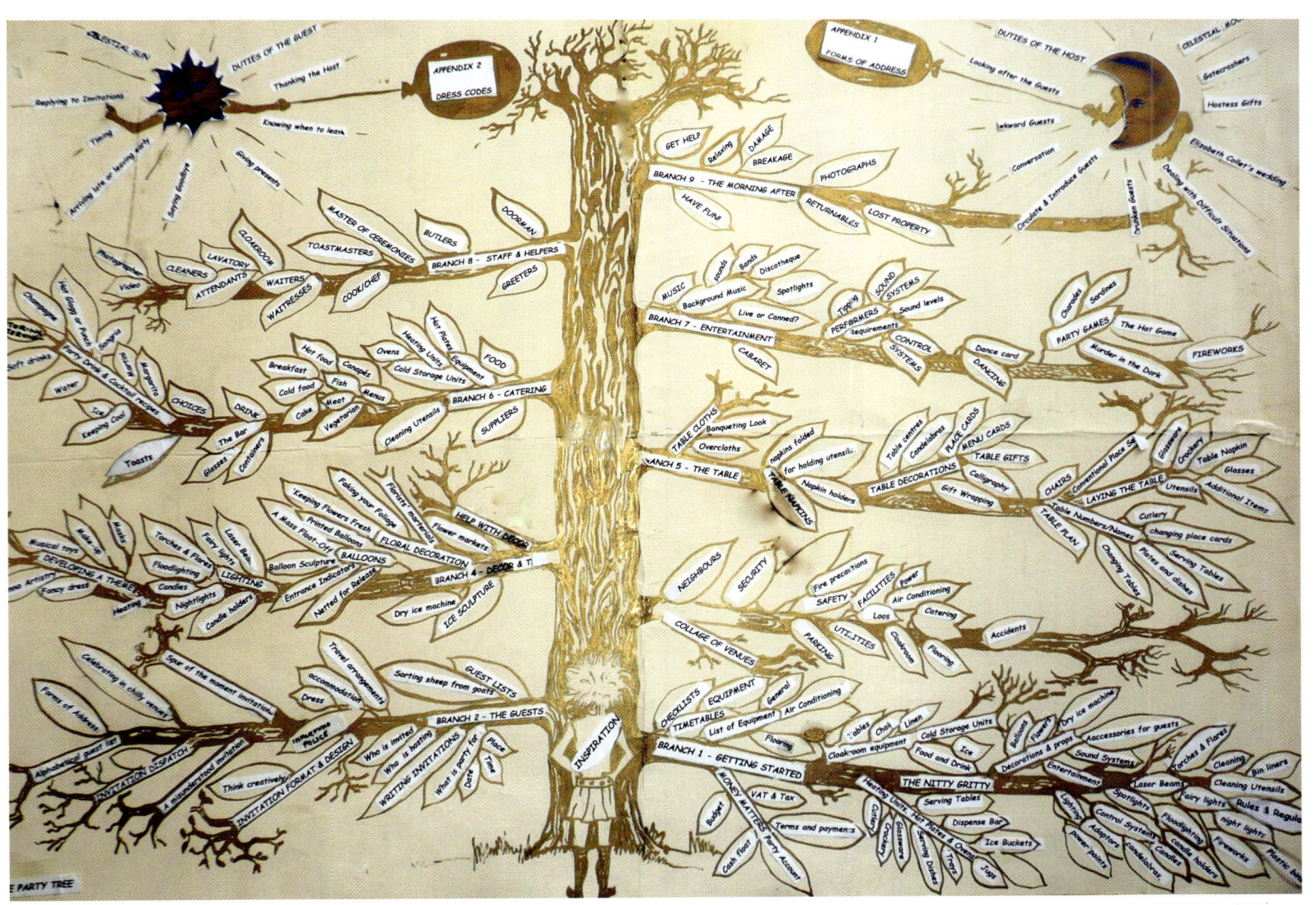

THE PARTY TREE

The modern definition of a party is: A social gathering of invited guests typically involving drinking, eating and entertainment, for pleasure and amusement for either celebration or promotion, and in today's world, often both!

introduction

When contemplating a party, uppermost in most people's minds are:

- BUDGET – borrow or buy!
  How much will it cost and how can I achieve the ultimate results with best value?
- LOCATION
  Where is the most appropriate, economical, and convenient venue?
- WHO TO INVITE – a private affair, or a mega fantasia created with and for a fistful of friends and acquaintances.
- WHAT THEY WISH TO ACHIEVE!

Over the past thirty years it has been my pleasure to answer these kind of questions for friends and clients, fulfilling their requests and desires, whilst bearing in mind budgets and all manner of bizarre ingredients. Occasionally when strapped for cash some of the more memorable occasions have been created with like souls, giving their time, energy and imagination, to achieve a memorable extravaganza with simple ingredients.

I adore parties and I love to create and organize them. I particularly enjoy the freedom they give to dress up, be with friends, and live out dreams with style and panache. Being able to enter a different world, divorced from the mundane reality of daily life, giving people the opportunity to satisfy their senses, remove barriers, socialize, communicate, and be themselves.

Planning a party is about creating that other world and it takes artistry, inventiveness, and the guts to be dashing, daring, but at the same time allowing consideration for people's feelings and sensitivities.

Over the years I have arranged countless parties in numerous locations, from the sandbanks of the Zambezi to mountain hideaways, private yachts, private islands, and sensational soirees in some of the most stately homes & historic establishments of Britain. My goal is to plan the first party in space, inspired by Buzz Aldrin who, with Neil Armstrong, was one of the first two astronauts to set foot on the moon!

During my life I have learnt that a significant celebration s not necessarily the sole right of the rich and famous and the amount of money spent not the yardstick by which to measure their success. An inventive host with a limited budget but good imagination and thought can achieve as much panache and magic as those with deeper pockets and more flexible budgets.

The secret of success in throwing perfect parties is the care and attention put into every detail in order to honour and delight the guests and enable the host to also have an enjoyable time.

I acquired my party-giving experience the hard way, learning through my mistakes. I learnt to be prepared for the unexpected to happen, as even the best plans don't always run smoothly.

Occasionally I hit problems, which appeared to be impossible to overcome, however there is usually a way of turning a minus into a plus. Retaining a sense of humour is paramount, even when things appear a disaster. There is generally a way out of even the darkest hole and often it is to start laughing. Laugh and all around hopefully will laugh with you. Cry and you'll resolve nothing.

In this, my second book on the subject, I will again share the knowledge and wisdom gained from my years of creating events, including the nuts and bolts, and do's and don'ts to achieve success on a more professional level. The shortcuts for maximum effect with minimum outlay with tips for negotiating every area of this complex and often frightening world of entertaining.

In this book I have added a chapter on etiquette, or rather modern day manners. A subject which I realise is greatly needed in today's hurried world.

Liz with Buzz Aldrin, who with Neil Armstrong was one of the first men on the moon, and Buzz's wife Lois.

Etiquette & modern day manners in the 21st century

social behaviour

Today, within practically every area of social behaviour, people are increasingly preoccupied in knowing what is considered the correct etiquette. Frankly, I believe manners are to do with making others feel comfortable and behaving in a way so as not to cause offence also certain ways of doing things generally tend to make life simpler.

A huge amount of nonsense has evolved with different cultures dictating to people, the right or wrong way of conducting oneself – from knowing which knife and fork to use to whether you pour the milk into the cup, before or after the tea, and so on and so forth.

I can assure the reader that nine times out of ten

where there is a rule there is a reason

and that reason is often simply common sense.

There are naturally traditions, which evolve and add charm to a culture and these need to be understood and respected for what they are, which is to a large extent part of our heritage.

It is tragic that we appear to be living in a culture, which is rapidly declining, as far as behaviour and language are concerned. Time and lack of it, is part of the cause, with people living increasingly frantic and stressful, busy lives.

At one time parents taught by setting an example and had time to sit as a family for meals, communicating and imparting knowledge. The schools and teachers, for whom this was an important part of education, shared this responsibility. They had the power to guide and instruct pupils concerning their general behaviour, manners, and language.

Now the inclination to do this has virtually disappeared, it is easier to turn a blind eye or ignore, hoping the young will eventually grow up and become worthwhile adults. They do, but sadly lacking the necessary grounding and sense of value.

Knowing where to start is a challenge. But for those who feel, as I do, that this is something which needs to be understood and appreciated, I have covered the areas which seem to be the main topics confusing people and where they may feel the need to master.

Liz teaching social behaviour and modern day manners ITV I 'Ladette to Lady'

SPEECH THERAPY, VOICE COACHING

which used to be referred to as elocution, is often controversial. People generally do not like to be criticised for the way they speak. I personally like regional accents, especially the soft lilt of an Irish accent. However, if an accent is so pronounced that the listener is incapable of understanding what is being said, then this needs to be addressed. I normally suggest people record their own voice and listen to how they speak. This is always a revealing exercise and it usually works. Once the speaker hears their own voice, as others do, they tend to want to improve their enunciation and tone.

Reading out loud is an excellent exercise as is repeating vowels, and phrases, even if you feel they are over accentuated. So although you may laugh and think the old 'How, now, brown cow' is absurdly ridiculous, as is 'The rain in Spain, falls mainly in the plain' – repeating those silly little ditties will in fact help!

POSTURE/DEPORTMENT

The way you stand or sit not only aids towards better health, especially with breathing, but also assists towards creating a more positive sense of presence, helping to give an impression of poise and elegance. The old fashioned walking around with books on the head may be laughable, but doing it a few times will make you aware of the degree you may need to alter your normal stance.

Sitting for long stretches of time at a computer can also damage posture and I strongly advise either a special stool or a chair designed specifically for this purpose.

MAKING A POSITIVE IMPRESSION & ACQUIRING SELF ESTEEM

There are enough self-help books on these subjects to encircle the earth. Basically you need to be aware of the power of your own thoughts and your personal energy. It has been my observation that the more people devour the contents of these books, the more insecure they become. Like an addictive drug, they continually seek yet another, more powerful solution, to fulfil an ever increasing need.

Stop thinking about yourself and concentrate on those around you or those you meet.

At all times choose to be positive. The alternative, being negative, accomplishes nothing.

A positive attitude and clear thinking, together with talking and visualizing with conviction, works wonders in gaining what you wish to achieve.

Everything begins in the mind. Nurture negativity and you will only succeed in becoming weak and success will have no chance. So train your mind to be decisive. Having courage and a positive attitude, will eventually give strength to your convictions and you will not only be a happier person but you are more likely to be healthier and have more energy.

Life is a matter of choices and you, and only you, are in charge of your life and taking steps to move in a successful and productive direction.

If you believe in yourself and your principles then don't be bullied into accepting something with which you disagree. Balance the pros and cons and if

Liz testing Lily Allen, Alan Carr and Justin Lee Collins on their elocution.
TV's Channel 4
'The Sunday Night Project' featuring Liz in their programme 'Chavette to Lady'

yours are what you consider correct then do not change your beliefs merely to conform to another's preferences.

Life does not always go according to your plan. Disappointments can influence your thoughts and cause disparity. At such times try and override your immediate feelings. If possible find some good, however small, that might emerge from what you consider is a disaster and bear in mind that laughter is a far more powerful tool than tears and helps to lighten a situation, enabling you to rise above it mentally.

BREAKING BAD HABITS

Bad habits prevent us from moving forward in our lives.

Three weeks is reputedly the time it takes to break a habit, and Aristotle taught, *"We are what we repeatedly do. Excellence, then, is not an act, but a habit"*.

To break a habit, first you have to come to terms with what you or those around you consider a bad habit. This can be the tedious repetition of meaningless words, i.e. the use of 'um' or 'you know', sniffing, wiping your nose on your sleeve, hogging the conversation, forgetting to say 'Thank you', drinking too much, biting your nails, being the last to leave, road rage, being too familiar etc.

The first step in breaking a habit is to accept that you have a problem, as nothing can change until your consciousness is made aware. Ask yourself what is the motivation, in other words, "why do I do it?" Then consider what may be the consequence. Having succeeded in getting this far then think about forming a new good habit to replace the bad one. At first try for a day, then a week and so on, at whatever pace suits you until you reach three weeks. If you slip off track, simply start again. Eventually you will be so aware of what you are doing you should succeed, but you must give this exercise a chance to work.

THE DIGITAL AGE

Over a decade into the 21st century and it is time for us to accept that the digital age is not only here to stay but also evolving at such a rate it is virtually impossible to keep pace, especially for the elderly.

The youth today no longer even wear watches! Their social lives are governed by digital networking and people's lives are speeding up to such an extent, we need to learn to actually switch off.

Decisions are made instantly and because we are able to do a huge amount more than a decade ago, we do, but not always for the best results.

Time has, for many of us, become a luxury and we need to introduce discipline and ease up. My advice is to take time to think before taking immediate action.

SOCIAL NETWORKING

A social network service is an online platform, a site that provides a service for people to connect and there are now active social networking websites operating in virtually every imaginable field. What do I think of them? I think they provide a valuable service but one that needs respect, understanding and control. At one time tracking past friends and acquaintances was hard work, now it is practically impossible to hide your identity, and finding people is easy. I sympathise though that it must be irritating for those who prefer to remain incognito.

Social networking should be used correctly and to your advantage, not, as it appears in many cases, that the person simply does not have a life. Reading some of the inane remarks being twittered around the world, however, it does make you wonder!

PERSONAL PRESENTATION

People assess you the moment you walk into a room. This, to a great extent is to do with your energy field, which, whether you are aware of it or not enters seconds before you and surrounds your being. The subconscious mind of the person or persons you are about to meet picks up on your energy and they form an instant opinion. Therefore when making an impression it is important to think positively, clear your mind of negative thoughts, take a deep breath, hold your head high, and smile! Then learn to listen attentively and think before you speak.

Having a positive attitude and taking care of how you present yourself, with attention to detail, is all-important and helps to make you feel more at ease, and confident, for example:

Heather Bird Tchenguiz showing how to relax on board!

- Clean healthy hair
- Manicured nails
- Wear clothes that flatter you and adapt fashions to suit your shape and personality.
- Smile!

DRESS SENSE

Dress sense is the art of knowing what is appropriate wear for different occasions and wearing what suits you, the life you live and your personality.

There is no myth attached, consider where you are going, what you will be doing and who you might be seeing or joining, then decide what would be the most sensible clothes and shoes. When in doubt take alternative shoes and something to either dress up or down what you are wearing and remember it is how you wear your clothes, not what you wear, that creates the effect. Subtlety is far sexier than showing too much cleavage! So be aware that a stylish backless evening gown sends a more significant message that exposing too much leg or décolleté and a subtly tailored slit skirt can be more alluring than a micro mini!

TABLE MANNERS

When you sit down at the dining table, put your table napkin on your lap. At the end of the meal you should leave your napkin crumpled – NOT folded, as it could be mistakenly re-used. When in doubt about how to eat a particular food either, Watch your host or other guests or use your common sense.

When being served a portion, don't be greedy; remember others also need to be served. In the UK, when you have finished eating, it is polite to place your utensils together to indicate you have finished. Do not eat too quickly, however you should not take so long you hold up the main course or the pudding.

Eating spaghetti

Wind a small amount neatly around the fork before putting it into your mouth. Some people do use a spoon to help, however, never do this in front of an Italian!

Eating bread before & during a meal

Break off enough bread from the bread roll for a mouthful at a time. Bread should be broken and not cut.

When to start eating

Do not begin eating before your host unless hot food has been served, in which case, wait a couple of minutes and then start eating. Your host wants you to appreciate the food and not let it get cold.

Eating

Do not speak with your mouth full. Do not make noises when eating your food or soup. If you need to remove something from your mouth use your spoon or fork to remove it.

Toothpicks

If it is absolutely necessary to use a tooth pick then do so discretely, hiding your mouth and the tooth pick behind your hand. Do this as quickly as possible. Do not use your fingers.

Note the charming way of presenting the orange on the fork

Similarly with lipstick, unless you decide to leave the table before the last course to touch up your make-up, be as discrete and as quick as possible. If you still feel awkward doing this at the table, then take a small dab of lipstick on your finger and dab it swiftly on your lips.

If you have to sneeze, turn your head away from the table and cover your nose with your handkerchief or, if you failed to remember your handkerchief then your napkin although you may receive disapproving glances!

Make certain you speak to people on either side of you. Seated at a more formal table the general rule is for the woman, seated between two men, to speak to the person on her right during the first course and to the man on her left during the second, then to whomever she chooses but not to leave one side mute for too long. If the table is very wide don't attempt to shout across to have a conversation, wait until afterwards or until after the pudding when things are generally more relaxed. If there is no particular placement then make certain those you are sitting near to are not ignored.

Do not eave the table until all guests have finished eating and the host indicates the meal is over. However if you have to use the bathroom, then excuse yourself and say you will be back in a minute.

FINANCIAL ETIQUETTE

Who pays for what, when?

Life has changed so dramatically over the past thirty years that, whereas at one time there were set rules as to who paid for what, whether in relation to dating, weddings, holidays, home etc. we now tend to treat this with a more modern attitude.

However, a woman still finds it unsexy paying the bills in a partnership, irrespective of circumstance.

RELATIONSHIPS

The break down in relationships and marriage could be partly due to the fact that men are less and less following their natural instinct to be the protectors and the providers. Men are biologically wired to procreate and therefore this is a natural instinct. Heterosexual men want to care for their woman and however emasculated and independent women may become I still believe most women melt when cherished and are made to feel like a woman. Men need to be allowed to be men. A woman's instinct is to create and run the home, and look after her man and family. Despite women in today's world excelling at multi-tasking, able to run a home, the social life, hold down a rewarding job, and have a hot meal ready at home for her partner or husband, unfortunately the trouble with life today is that our lives are all speeding up and everything happens too fast. Time is becoming the greatest luxury and we need to take time to relax, slow down, and communicate better.

KISSING/GREETING/SAYING GOODBYE

Invading personal space – this is something which has slipped into the behaviour

"Where have all the young men gone?"
Liz seated at
Andrew Granville Douglas Gordon's
dining table in his Balinese style villa
at Tryall, Jamaica

pattern of the last few years. When meeting someone for the first time I find it inappropriate for that person to feel that they have the right to be familiar and kiss me on both cheeks or hug me. Actually it is that energy field, or aura around me (and you), which really objects! To invade personal space should be a gradual and gentle process and not taken for granted the first time two people meet.

We each have this unique aura around us, similar to an energy field and my subconscious being takes exception to someone I do not know penetrating my personal protective space. To avoid this, as charmingly and politely as I can, I put out my hand to shake theirs and hopefully stop their invasion.

Saying goodbye is something the English are almost incapable of doing quickly. It is almost a ritual; from the moment that you or a guest decides to leave saying goodbye takes forever. But that is the English way and it is what it is!

MOBILE PHONES

It is OK to SWITCH OFF!

Consider what your ringtone says about you. If in doubt – change the tune and monitor the volume.

I always remember years ago when I was launching Special Olympics Great Britain with a Cocktail party at Downing Street followed by dinner at the Foreign Office, right in the middle of the host's speech, actress Leslie Joseph's mobile shrieked the never to be forgotten inimitable tune of 'Scotland the brave!'

Always be aware when your phone should be turned off. If you continually make mistakes then have it permanently on vibrate!

Speak quietly. It is quite extraordinary how many people give no consideration to others who have no interest in hearing your phone conversation, especially on public transport or public places.

If you are in a situation when you cannot use your phone, live with it – life will continue!

When meeting a friend for a meal, keep your phone in your pocket on vibrate. Do not put it on the table. Sharing your time between your friends/colleagues and mobile is inconsiderate and makes it difficult for you and those around to concentrate.

Nancy Dell'Olio demonstrates how to keep others from invading her private space at Liz's Luncheon hosted by George Piskov at Royal Ascot

Liz greeting Nancy Dell'Olio

Nancy Dell'Olio greeting Lady Henrietta Rous and Billy Adlington

If you are expecting an urgent call during a social occasion, forewarn your guest or host, apologizing in advance. Then remove yourself and take the call in private.

A good friend of mine continually complains that people bump into him walking along the street whilst on their mobile. I agree this happens all too often and is not only dangerous but also annoying, especially when crossing roads.

ANSWERING INVITATIONS

RSVP means the host expects a reply! So please REPLY !

It amazes me how many people do not answer an invitation. How is the exasperated host expected to cater without knowing the number of attendees?

Leaving your reply to the last minute is only an indication that you are hoping for a better invitation! NOT replying to an invitation and turning up deserves the door to remain firmly closed. If possible, make a habit of replying immediately. If something unavoidable happens you can then contact your host and explain giving them hopefully a chance to replace you.

THANKING

If you have gone to the trouble of entertaining, sending a present, or doing a personal deed then consider how you might feel if the result is silence! How you show thanks is up to you, but bear in mind a meaningful card, personal call, or flowers, shows you have taken time and consideration, which is far more impressive than a mere text! Hand-written letters are so rare nowadays they will become collectors' items – however nothing is more effective.

Baron Burca escorts Lady Colin Campbell as Marco di Cesaria greets her in the European way at Royal Ascot

Chris & Caro Hacking's Birthday
celebrations in the gardens adjacent to
their Chelsea home, London, showing
their impeccable table plan. Fortunately
all the guests replied and there were
no empty chairs!

how to achieve a memorable occasion

party planning

dream the event

'Let's have a party!'' someone exclaims and everyone replies, 'What a great idea 'Let's have a party!' Suddenly there is a delicious tingle in the air, a feeling of expectancy that something exciting is about to happen.

In between this first great burst of enthusiasm and the moment the last guest departs, there is an ocean of uncharted waters. At first calm and easy to navigate but soon filled with unforeseen perils that need a steady hand at the helm.

The secret of how to start is to dream the event in your mind. Dream your perfect party and let your imagination run wild. Start at the beginning and cover every detail and eventuality.

At this embryonic stage, your idea is like a tiny seed, and a long way from complete form.

There are so many things to consider. So to avoid panic attacks I created the PARTY TREE on page 11 after the Contents. Each branch represents a significant ingredient brimming with an assortment of ideas and requirements for bringing people together to enjoy a significant event.

The secret is to dream.........

'Whatever you can do or dream, you can begin it... boldness has genius, power and magic in it'

GOETHE

branch 1

getting started - the nitty-gritty

MONEY MATTERS

Budget

Draw up an approximate budget covering all the obvious outgoings. Sift through the pages of this book having studied the PARTY TREE, at the beginning and make a checklist of all the necessary ingredients and items required.

Make provision for hidden extras and be aware that when you receive a quote it does not always include VAT.

If you find the anticipated costs exceed your planned budget you will need to either:

- Revise the budget
- Compromise on the details
- Be prepared to improvise (some of the ways are described in this book) so that you can minimize costs

Bear in mind that buying in bulk is more economical and non-perishable items can always be reserved for future events. It is also worth talking to your various suppliers to negotiate discounts and or a 'sale or return' arrangement wherever possible, especially for large orders.

Having decided your budget, you may find it an advantage – especially if you are planning a large event – to open a separate bank account to use solely for party expenditure. This will give you a more accurate picture of how the finances are going as you proceed

EQUIPMENT

Deciding what equipment you will need is a very tedious part of organising parties, but it is vitally important and must be taken seriously, if no essential detail is to be overlooked.

The caterers usually provide banqueting equipment. If a marquee is being used, they can also provide tables, chairs, and portable flooring, however, if you decide to do your own catering then, with large numbers, hiring equipment makes sense. Some catering companies will advise and supply your needs even if they are not providing the food and drink. Nowadays, many restaurants also hire out crockery and other utensils; the leaders have some stylish selections superior to the normal canteen-type ware. Of course, if you are organising a 'Bad Taste' Party such as friends of mine did for their 50th birthday several years ago, you will not be seeking stylish accoutrements!

CHECKLIST OF EQUIPMENT

General
    Air conditioning units
    Industrial heaters
    Portable flooring (if there is no dance floor at the chosen venue)
    Cloakroom equipment and lavatory accessories

Food & drink

Tables & chairs
Serving tables
Linen – if using table cloths, table napkins
Cold storage units
Heating units/hot plates/ovens
Crockery
Cutlery
Glasses
Jugs
Serving dishes
Ice buckets
Containers
Trays
Dispense bar

Decorations & props

Balloons
Flowers, plants, trees
Fancy dress accessories (make-up, hats etc)
Assorted Décor

Lighting & sound equipment

Control systems/sound systems
Adaptors/ extensions leads
Spotlights
Laser beams
Torches and flares
Fairy lights
Floodlighting
Candles, candle holders, candelabras
Nightlights
Fireworks

WRITE IT DOWN!

It is amazing how many little items are overlooked or forgotten. So keep a notepad on you at all times and whenever you think of something important, write it down. You may well find that, like me, you end up writing lists of lists, but at least you will not keep worrying about what you might be forgetting.

Cleaning

Selection of cloths, kitchen towels
Cleaning products
Dustpan & Brush
Mop, broom, vacuum cleaner etc
Plastic bins and plenty of bin liners

RULES & REGULATIONS

Responsibilities

The serious part of organizing a large event is that you must ensure compliance with relevant legislation, to ensure the safety of everyone working or attending your event.

You need to contact all the relevant authorities if you are using a location not normally used as a venue, to check you will not breach any rules or regulations. It is important to find out early in the planning stage what you need to comply with, as the information may affect your decision to use that particular venue.

For example, there may be restrictions on the numbers of attendees, musicians, or entertainers permitted to perform. Special licences are likely if the occasion is a form of fund-raisers with people buying entrance tickets. The authorities can also guide you on a number of other points including:

- Licensing hours
- Minimum facilities required for the number of guests
- Noise levels
- Rubbish collection
- Fire regulations
- First Aid
- Food Safety

'The morning after the night before' – a clean sweep after another great evening staying with Meriel and Patrick White at their house-party in St Tropez.

Contact the licensing department at the Town Hall

Even when hiring an established licensed venue, check the licensing hours. It is possible that the owner, licensee or you will have to apply for an extension to the hours or a Temporary Event Notice, in order that dancing and drinking can continue after the normal licensing hours. Check also that the venue is licensed for performing artists.

Health & safety

A Guide to Health, Safety and Welfare at Music or similar events can be requested from the local Council.

Planning & notice

If possible start the practical organizing well before the event, giving you time to carry out risk assessments and obtain specialist advice where necessary.

It will also allow time for the authorities (police, fire, ambulance & council) to make relevant arrangements, especially if they need to attend the event. Also common sense is required. No one likes queuing for the loo so make certain you have enough and they are clearly marked and fully equipped!

A great party is the result of a clever mix of Sugar & Spice!

LIZ BREWER

branch 2

guests & invitations

A good mixture of guests is an important ingredient to help in accomplishing the success of a memorable event. Guests who are all of a kind can be dull; so don't avoid adding some personable sugar and spice to the Guest List.

Think carefully about whom you would like to invite, after all, most people hope to share special occasions with interesting and amusing friends.

Choose those who you really want as guests, ones who contribute to an occasion and enhance the atmosphere by injecting their vitality. Sociable, animated guests help create the party of parties and memories which last. There is little point in inviting known party bores, even if you feel obliged to include them to return past hospitality, for the sake of the success of your party, do so at another time.

GUEST LISTS

Create a list of guests from different categories. When I do this, I generally end up with ten times too many guests, so a great deal of diplomatic pruning has to be done.

"Let's get this party started."

COLLAGE OF GUESTS
at Dame Shirley's Birthday party at
Cliveden House, Taplow, Berkshire

- Peter de Savary
- Dame Shirley Bassey
  escorted by
  Christopher Biggins as Santa
  and some 'fancy boys'
- Martin Brewer & Penny Lee
- Lisa Voice
- Toyah Wilcox & John Wayne
- The Invitation card for
  Dame Shirley Bassey's
  Birthday party at
  Cliveden House
- George & Tanya Piskov
  with sons Peter & Egor
- The four members of BLAKE,
  winners of Classic Album of
  the year, who wheeled in
  the cake!
- Liz with
  Mona Bauwens Al-Ghussein
  and Louise Kornfeld

- Joan Collins, Dame Shirley
  and Percy Gibson
- The entertainers
  outside Cliveden
- Tallulah Rendall who sang
  'The Living Tree'
- Bruce & Wilnelia Forsyth
- Rolf Harris
- Ben Duncan with a couple
  of decorative girls
- Lyn Schlesinger &
  Hamish Scott
- Dame Shirley, Cilla Black
  & Christopher Biggins
- The Party's over! Liz,
  Andrew Davis, Chairman of
  von Essen Hotels, who hosted
  the party at Cliveden and
  Dame Shirley fly home
  in one of Andrew's
  Premier Air helicopters

Liz & Aline Hay of Duns with Elvis Presley? He may only be a cut out but he's certainly a talking point!

Compile your list from:

- Family and good friends
- Singles and couples
- Sugar & spice
- Young and old fun-loving wrinklies!
- Personalities

For a significant event, a good tip is to check in advance, either by phone, text or email your important guest's availability before sending out invitations. As you receive the feedback you will find you will be in a position to adjust your list accordingly and start to include the second level of guests. At this advanced stage it is advisable to send a 'Save the Date' notification before sending the official invitation.

Making your guest list more exciting

A cunning trick to make your guest list more exciting is to inject new blood.

E.g. invite a neighbour you have not met or someone you would like to know but not had the opportunity to meet. With a special occasion, an unexpected invitation is likely to be welcomed with a surprising level of good will and curiosity.

Sugar & Spice

I really enjoy mixing people and frequently invite varied and unusual guests as this normally creates indelible memories.

If your guest list looks somewhat dull, put your invited guests to work and suggest they bring a new or fascinating friend who could be a valuable addition to add extra zing and razzmatazz to your gathering. Flatter them by saying something like,

'You always have such interesting people around you – let me know if there is someone you might like to bring along'.

Announcing your party on Facebook or other social networking tool is inadvisable unless you are organizing an event, which is not private, or something, which needs public awareness.

Singles

It is your prerogative to decide whether you invite your guests with or without suggesting they bring a friend. However, be tactful and never presume a single person wants to come alone. Often, unless you specify to bring a guest, they will assume they have been asked singly to balance the numbers, so if your numbers allow, check to see if there is someone who they would particularly like to accompany them, but make certain they supply the name. Two reasons for this: First it could be catastrophic if this was someone you already knew and for whatever reason you would not wish to attend. Secondly you need to be in a position to make necessary introductions (see 'duties of the host').

Alphabetical order

Always create your guest list with the SURNAMES in alphabetical order.
It continually surprises me how often people omit doing this, as it is such an easy method and will save considerable time and confusion.
Computers have the ability to handle this.

Sorting the sheep from the goats

Number of invitations

If you are having invitations printed it is better to order too many than find you have not enough. As a general rule I print double the number of invitations I require, so for 100 guests I order 200 invitations. You will discover the extra cost per hundred is minimal, and it is amazing how quickly they get used. Also there are often a number of people to whom you wish to send the invitation despite knowing they are unable to attend. I always consider, it is after all, flattering to be asked!

Sorting the sheep from the goats!

Split your guest list into an A & B list. Mail the A list first and as the inevitable polite refusal arrives, you will already be prepared with alternative guests to invite. This may sound callous but at times it is a necessity.

WRITING INVITATIONS

The traditional invitation card is the simplest and most informative way of providing

Grayson Perry at the
House of Lords in his party
frock with Cindy Jackson & Liz.

guests with all the relevant details they may require.

HOWEVER the standard invitation format is not set in stone, so, don't feel the need to be bullied by convention, so long as you remember to include ALL necessary details then design and wording is up to you.

Celebrations, events, and parties have hugely multiplied since the middle of the last century. Thus securing the 'Hot ticket' tag to an invitation has become increasingly competitive and therefore, in recent years, invitations have become ever more original and inventive. The implication being, the more inventive, or inspiring the design, the more interesting the party. This is not necessarily the case, although original, impressive invitations generally do have the desired impact.

Buckingham Palace &
Highgrove invitations, menus,
table cards & place cards

It is imperative to cover all the basic facts

For this reason the basic wording of the so-called 'formal invitation' is often the easiest and simplest guide: the wording suits the purpose and it is foolproof.

Save the date or pour memoir card

This is a wise and useful small card to send if your have invited guests by phone email or text. It's my experience, in this electronic age, that people with busy lives often overlook an invitation, unless, what's still occasionally referred to as a 'Stiffy' is received. For young readers a 'stiffy' is an invitation printed on hard card!

As this is a reminder, the RSVP bearing your telephone number is printed but crossed out (but not omitted in case the guest has any queries) indicating that you have already received their verbal or text/email reply.

Mrs Liz Brewer

Requests the pleasure of the company of
Mr & or Mrs/Ms/Miss Suitable guest's name
To celebrate her birthday
On Wednesday 6th June 2012
at
Annabel's Berkeley Square, London, W1J 5AR

RSVP
21 Fantasy Road
London SW1 XXX
email: liz.brewer@fantasy.com
Tel: XX XXXX XXXX

Dress: Black Tie
Dinner: 8pm for 8.30pm
Carriages: 1.00am

Please bring this invitation card with you

A standard formal
Invitation card
NOTE – The name of
the guest should be
handwritten in ink

Suitable guest's name
(handwritten in ink)

Liz Brewer

Requests the pleasure of your company
To celebrate her birthday
On Wednesday 6th June 2012
at
Annabel's Berkeley Square, London, W1J 5AR

Regrets only:
21 Fantasy Road
London SW1 XXX
email: liz.brewer@fantasy.com
Tel: XX XXXX XXXX

Dress: Black Tie
Dinner: 8pm for 8.30pm
Carriages: 1.00am

Please bring this invitation card with you

A less formal
version of the
standard invitation.

43

Private Jet or even
Helicopters at Noon!!

Giving the Post Code and
good directions saves guests
the frustration of getting lost!

The basic facts which must be included are:

- Name of the host
- Name of the guest (written by hand)
- Purpose of the event (if any)
- Date
- Time of arrival
- Time to depart
- Place
- Dress code
- Food & drink provision
- RSVP or Reply to: Name and address, email or telephone number to whom replies should be made
- For security reasons 'Please bring this invitation with you' can be printed at the bottom and it does help deter gatecrashers

Name of the host

The most appropriate place for the host's name is at the top of whatever it is you choose to use for the invitation.

Name of the guest

Handwritten in either the top left-hand corner or on its own on a separate line, depending on the format and design of the invitation. You should also indicate whether you are asking the guest to come alone or with his/her partner or with a guest of his/her choice. Hopefully the invitee will reply accordingly if not you need to find out the name of their guest.

Purpose of the event, if any

Forewarn guests by stating clearly the reason for the celebration. If there is a 'guest of honour', this should be made clear. The idea of having a 'guest of honour' gives an excellent reason for having a party.

Suitable guest's name
(name handwritten)

Liz Brewer

*Requests that you reserve Saturday 20th September
2012 to celebrate her daughter Tallulah Rendall's
birthday, on Cortes Island British Columbia*

Formal Invitation to follow

(Print or write here whatever contact
details you wish to provide)
liz.brewer@fantasy.com

'SAVE THE DATE'
card

Suitable Guest
(hand-written)

*Please save the date, Saturday 20th September
2012 to join us in celebrating my daughter
Tallulah Rendall's birthday on
Cortes Island, British Columbia.*

Invitation to follow.

Liz Brewer
Mobile: xxxxx xxxxxx
(or whatever contact details you
wish to include.)

An alternative
'SAVE THE DATE'

The 'POUR MEMOIR' or
'REMINDER' Card

Liz Brewer

Thanksgiving Luncheon
Mosimann's Club
11b West Halkin Street
London SW1 8JB

Thursday 24th November 2011

'Pour Memoir'
Tel: 020 0000 0000 (crossed out)
(Thus indicating it is unnecessary to
call, unless for an important reason)

Dress: Stars & Stripes!
12.30 for 1pm

AT HOME CARD
Useful for any type of
entertaining at home. Simply
write the name of the guest
in the top left hand corner,
the details of what you are
organising in the centre, plus, the
time and, if necessary, the dress
code, bottom right.

Liz Brewer

At home

R.S.V.P.
21 Fantasy Road
London, SW1X XXX
020 XXXX XXXX
liz.brewer@fantasy.com

Date

Important to include the day of the week as well as the date. This makes it doubly clear when the event is and helps to cement the date in the guest's mind.

Time of arrival and departure

Be aware that very few people arrive at the time stipulated. Generally guests arrive fifteen to thirty minutes after the time indicated, unless the host states 'From 8pm' (or whatever), in which case the guest has more choice.

Always indicate the departure time, unless you are prepared for guests to overstay their welcome and you end up with a mammoth 'sleep-over'! Something along the following lines written on the bottom right of the invitation card, gives a clear message:

Carriages, or anything fun such as rickshaws, magic carpets, flying saucers, private jets, walking shoes (or whatever else your imagination conjures up!) at midnight (or whatever time you decide).

Place

State NAME & ADDRESS of venue INCLUDING THE POST CODE for navigation systems. If necessary print a map on the reverse of the invitation or enclose directions and, or a map, on a separate sheet. Trust me there are still people who manage to get lost!

Information on PARKING facilities is also helpful.

Travel arrangements and accomodation

Consider those who may have to travel considerable distances to join you. These people do you a great compliment by making the effort to attend, therefore give consideration to how they travel and where they might stay to suit all pockets.

Include info on bed & breakfasts as well as local hotels and perhaps friends who could be willing to overnight special guests.

List trains & the local station, taxi, or limousine services, car hire and when appropriate flight information.

Cary Arms Taxi

Kevin Spacey & Liz with friends in electric cart at the 'Ivan The Terrible' Polo event

White Tie & Tails – the grounds of Eggleston Hall, County Durham

Christopher Buxton OBE in Nehru style evening Jacket

DRESS

Celebrating in chilly venues

especially Scottish castles!

Whatever the venue, a chill in the air will make thin bloods feel uncomfortable and unhappy. If the temperature is likely to be cold, advise guests beforehand – either with an amusing addendum to the invitation (Dress: Black Tie and thermal underwear!) There is nothing worse than feeling cold. It induces frosty moods and matching memories of the occasion. Far better to be honest and avoid criticism.

Convention dictates specific dress for certain occasions and although this is fairly universal, Britain does tend to take this more seriously, however in turn, it adds to the charisma of the country. Tradition is after all tradition and albeit at times quaint, it should where possible be respected and adhered to.

A guide to dress codes is given later in the book, however, in general, when the host decides on a dress code, it is important to bear in mind that clothes should suit the occasion and above all be comfortable and appropriate. A Black Tie candle-lit picnic in the open air can be enchanting, so long as the weather doesn't put a damper on the occasion. Black Tie at a barn dance could prove awkward and uncomfortable.

So when deciding on the dress code, use your common sense. It is, however, your event and you can dictate. Bear in mind, though, that a special occasion deserves more attention when it comes to dress. It is not every day you throw a significant party so it is worth asking your guests to make more of an effort.

At a private function, as against a corporate event, you are the boss and therefore you can allow your guests a certain amount of leverage. Nowadays there is a tendency towards individual expression as against the conventional uniform type of dress. Frequently at Black Tie events men are making a quiet statement with Nehru jackets, black silk roll-neck shirts, or even designer black T-shirts.

Go back two or three hundred years and men dressed flamboyantly with their powdered wigs, ruffles, and dandyish appearance. Bring it on, say I!

Whatever you decide concerning the dress code, indicate it clearly on the invitation.

Normally the Dress Code is placed at the bottom right side of the card.

Simply stating 'Evening dress' or 'Formal' is not good enough and will only result in tedious enquiries as to 'How formal', 'does that mean long or short'? Is that black tie or white tie? Etc.

Suitable footwear

If the occasion takes place outdoors or on a boat, take care to warn guests concerning footwear. On board SHOELESS is strictly 'de rigueur', in order to protect the decks. Unless stated otherwise shoes are normally removed and placed in a basket/box before alighting on deck. Lenient owners allow rope or rubber soles whilst on more commercial boats, used for banqueting purposes, shoes are generally not a problem.

High heels are uncomfortable on grass and look out of place on a polo ground or lawn at a garden party.

If, as a guest, you are uncertain what footwear would be most appropriate, take a pair of either more practical, or more elegant shoes (whichever the case) in a shoe bag so that you are prepared. There is nothing worse than wearing shoes that are unsuitable or uncomfortable.

Food or drink provision

Normally this is written either above or below the Dress code bottom right of the card.

Letting the guest know what is being provided is a necessary consideration so they know whether or not they will be fed and what type of drink is being served.
e.g. 7.30pm Champagne reception
8.00pm Seated Dinner
or
Cocktails from 6pm
Followed by Buffet
or
7.30 for 8pm which means drinks before dinner
or even a very casual:
7pm Drinks
9pm Food

Shoes on the harbour wall! Ivana Trump reckons she can judge the quality of the party on a yacht, by the Shoe line up!!

RSVP or Reply to

This is important and normally written on the bottom left of the invitation. State clearly name, address, email, telephone/mobile or whatever method you like so long as it is clear they need to respond.

In today's world all these methods are acceptable.

INVITATION FORMAT & DESIGN

There are no hard and fast rules on the size of an invitation. Practicalities though, frequently dictate.

It is obviously simpler and more economical to stick to a size, which suits the conventional sized envelope.

Formal invitations are generally 18 x 12.5cm or 10 x 7.5cm and die cast, although this tradition is fast disappearing. I must admit I still pass my thumb over an invitation to check! 'At Home' cards, available from most stationers, are pre-printed and convenient to use for dinner parties, drinks or cocktail parties. If in doubt about the size or style, pop along to your local printer and look through his sample books.

Today with the ever-increasing developments of technology it is not difficult to produce your own invitations at home or at least prepare your own artwork ready for the printer. It goes without saying that the proof needs VERY CAREFUL checking so all the necessary information is CORRECT!

Think creatively

Designing invitations gives you a wonderful opportunity to dream up unusual and artistic ideas. Experiment! Let the kids help. Children's minds have a freshness that gives them the knack of adding spontaneity to a design. Or get together with a friend – two minds inevitably work better than one.

If all else fails get your printer to recommend a good graphic designer. Explain exactly what is required and get a quote.

Over the years I have created numerous invitations and always enjoyed creating something new and unusual.

I learnt an indelible lesson early in my career that an ingenious, unusual, and impressive invitation could work miracles. It was to launch one of Brian Stein's original hamburger restaurants in Covent Garden, London. All the odds were against this being a success, however after many hours Brian persuaded me. That night I was unable to sleep, worrying. Finally at 4am I wrote to Brian explaining how guilty I'd feel taking the high fee – which I would still charge.

I again explained to him:

Launching hamburger restaurants was definitely not my forté
Early September, was not a good time.
Everyone I knew was away.
AND above all I really didn't know this market.

I hand-delivered the letter to his Hampstead address at 5am only to be woken at 8am by Brian returning my letter, telling me that I could not go back on my word. He charmingly assured me that even if no one turned up, I had to do the party! So, convinced that most people would not appear I trebled the guest list and went into overdrive. I even invited a few pearly kings and queens for good measure.

The invitation was designed to pop up into a 3D cutout image of the restaurant. It was Brian's creation and it was brilliant.

A miracle happened and I can only imagine that invitees returning from their holidays, feeling in a party mood looking healthy and tanned, combined with the remarkable and persuasive invitation did the trick, as over 500 guests turned up! How Brian's restaurant coped, I'll never know, but everyone was fed and the champagne flowed. The only tragedy was a couple of Bentleys and three Rolls Royce cars were towed away, including Marvin Gaye's – the driver having gone off for a quick bite. This hit the headlines and suffice to say I don't think Brian every looked back!

The Marquess of Bath and Liz

A misunderstood invitation

When dreaming up innovative and unusual invitations, there is naturally the risk that they may misfire. When I had the privilege of organizing the centenary celebration of one of the world's leading caviar suppliers, the idea was to launch Caviar Soup. I arranged a seated dinner for twenty-two celebrity guests at Mosimann's Dining Club in London's Belgravia. The invitation was written on individual small scrolls of paper, embedded into fake caviar in empty Beluga Caviar tins. I created the fake caviar from grey stained polystyrene balls.

The invitations were mailed and I awaited the replies. Receiving a call from the Wessex constabulary took me by surprise. It appears the entire local bomb squad had been summoned in force to Longleat House, home of the Marquess of Bath, by a worried butler who assumed that his Lordship's invitation contained a bomb!

It felt like one, rattled like one, and was especially suspicious; I had to contend with an irate police officer demanding to know what I was up to!

Spur of the moment invitation

Occasionally, when deciding to organize a spur of the moment event, I have really had to stretch my imagination. A private celebrity pre-Christmas dinner, seated for thirty, I was asked to host with a week's notice, needed something striking fast, so I created the invitation and tucked it inside a simple Christmas Cracker to which I added some additional glamour. Then I had them hand-delivered with a message saying 'PULL IMMEDIATELY'. Every invited guest attended and they still comment on the invitation.

Another time I stuck a tiny piece of mistletoe on the top of the invitation. This also achieved an equally successful result however they fitted more easily into a normal large envelope and could be posted.

Last minute invitations are fun and often successful. If the sun is shining and you decide to gather friends to have an instant picnic in your garden or somewhere enticing then go for it.

INVITATION DISPATCH & REPLY

Check and doubly check the addresses and postcodes. The 21st-century Royal Mail is not that co-operative and often if there are mistakes with the code or address the invitations do not get delivered.

Also if the postage is incorrect the receiver has the bore of having to pay excess and this makes a bad impression.

There are no strict rules dictating how far in advance invitations should be sent, but the following could help as a guideline:

- Important occasions, such as weddings, special anniversaries or significant birthdays give as much notice as possible with a 'Save the Date' communication. Six months to a year in advance is not out of order. Then make certain the actual invitation is sent at least six weeks in advance.
- If a significant invitation is made over the phone or through another means of communication make certain you follow up with a reminder, either by text, email, or pour memoir card.
- For Charity events one to four months with a reminder nearer the date unless you are having a problem filling seats in which case personal phone calls, electronic messages, Twitter or Facebook etc may help but don't overdo this. There is nothing more annoying than being pestered to buy tickets to an event which you have no intention of attending.
- Normal Cocktail party three to six weeks is fine.
- Significant dinner party three to six weeks + is in order.
- Informal invitations made with phone, emailed, text or other type of communication are more flexible with times, although an announcement is normally made a few days or weeks in advance with a reminder sent to arrive a day or two before.
- As you receive replies, immediately note the acceptances and refusals on your main guest list. If the replies are written, this is a good opportunity to cross check with your database to make certain their data information is correct.
- Once you get an idea of the numbers attending, or unable to attend, act swiftly to substitute replacement guests if necessary.

it will be appreciated. Correct forms of address usually depend on your degree of friendship. If you are inviting a mere acquaintance and not sure how someone is styled, either check wikipedia the free on line encyclopaedia, a copy of 'Whitaker's Almanac' or Who's Who and stick to the formal address. A brief guide to formal styles of address are also shown later in the book.

'*Imagine all the people*'

JOHN LENNON

Imagine

branch 3

venue

Choice of venue is very much a personal decision influenced by budget, number of attendees, convenience, and what would give you and your guests the most amount of pleasure. Normally, the initial contact for your reservation/booking should be made through the appropriate authority – e.g. the banqueting manager, general manager, or owner.

With popular venues, availability can be a problem, so it is wise to reserve, well in advance. If the date you have in mind is not available, do not be disheartened, as there are always alternatives. To ignite your imagination, I have listed a se ection of possibilities to ponder. This is a fairly random, some might think rid culous list however by glancing over these, your mind may well trigger an appropriate alternative location.

Having selected some possibilities and confirmed their availability, you need to start looking into their viability. Weigh up the pros and cons and suitability of each one, taking as many details as possible into consideration and start preparing a feasibility study and cost analysis. This is also the time to begin bargaining with the various powers that be, in order to get the most attractive deal.

VENUES

- Top deck on
  Terence Cole's Yacht
- Holland & Holland's
  dining lodge
- Stephen Kornfeld's Bar-b-q
- John & Eileen Outerbridge
  in Bermuda
- Penny Lee's conservatory
  in Surrey
- Overlooking the sea
  in Jamaica at
  The Sugar Cane Ball
  Roundhill
- Brian Lown's Fishing party
  on the Test
- Baron Hamer's Box,
  Henley Regatta
- Dickie Thirlby at home
  with Caviar!
- Concert supper in my
  Belgravia garden, London
- The Throne Room,
  Buckingham Palace!

- Mark Law's old Gallery
  in Bond Street
- Manderston the home of
  Lord & Lady Palmer
  Liz in the grip of their
  famous bear
- Dame Shirley Bassey,
  Nicolo Mirabile Di Ziltc,
  & Niki Cole at the
  Hotel de Paris, Monte Carlo
- Liz with Ivana Trump &
  Theresa Roberts at her
  Jamaican home,
  Hanover Grange, Tryall
- The dining room at
  Cliveden House, Taplow
- The dining room at
  Duns Castle
- A dining room in Moscow
- Ian & Victoria Watson's dining
  room in St Leonards Terrace,
  London.

possible venues

Airport/Heliport
Amusement park
Art Gallery
Attic
Ballroom
Banqueting hall
Bar
Barge
Barrel room
Barn
Beach
Boat

Boat yard
Bus
Car park
Castle
Caves
Church hall
Circus
Cinema
College hall
Concert hall
Conservatory
Country club
Dance hall
Deck
Desert
Desert Island
Discotheque
Dungeons
Exhibition hall
Factory
Fairground
Farm
Ferry
Film studio
Flotilla
Forest
Garden
Garage
Harbour
Health Spa
Hospital

Hot-air balloon
Hotel
Hot tub
In bed –
    slumber party!
Lagoon
Lake
Lighthouse
Livery hall
Marquee
Members club
Mountains
Museum
Night club
Opera house
Palace
Park
Pavilion
Pier
Planetarium
Playground
Polo ground
Private house
Pub
Race course
Race track
Restaurant
Retirement home
Roof
Ruins
Safari camp

Sailing ship
School
Ship
Shop
Space station
Square
Stables
Stadium
Stately home
Station
Steam train
Street
Studio
Submarine
Swimming pool
Temple
Tent – Arabian,
    Moroccan, plain
    army etc
Tepee
Theatre even backstage!
Tower
Town hall
Train
Vineyard
Waxwork museum
Winery
Yacht
Yacht club
Zoo

NEIGHBOURS

If you are celebrating at home or at a friend's house, it is polite and a good idea to forewarn your neighbours, especially if they are not being invited. The last thing you want is complaints about noise or badly parked cars. Alerting them will at least, give them fair warning and this could help to diffuse annoyance, which might otherwise result in an unpleasant incident or unsympathetic and aggressive reaction. Frankly, if you are planning a large party it saves an awful lot of bother just to include the neighbours.

SAFETY & SECURITY

A Great Venue, Duns Castle on the borders of Scotland, home of Alick & Aline Hay of Duns & family. (Plus Marquee)

One thing you will never regret paying particular attention to is security. Increased activity with people coming and going, delivering and collecting, is an open invitation to thieves. A friend of mine, the morning after a fabulous party, gratefully let in a team to clear the contents of the marquee, including all the hired equipment, left-over supplies, hired crystal and china etc. They did a superb job: nothing remained. Only problem was, half an hour later the real caterers arrived!

To avoid such disasters it is well worth finding a capable person to take responsibility for the security before and after the event.

Strict security on the entrance is vital. Uninvited guests can be extremely annoying and it is best to keep them – and any other undesirables, from entering. Much will depend on the event, however, as a general rule a reliable security firm or a person who is aware of the problems that may arise should do this important job.

Fire precautions

You have a responsibility towards your guests therefore safety precautions are a necessity to be taken seriously, especially concerning fire.

Fabric MUST be fireproof. This includes marquee linings, tablecloths, chair-covers, and all soft furnishings. Candles easily fall and ignite fabric. Even light fittings can overheat and cause fire. Small household fire extinguishers should be at hand in every home. For a large event, it is imperative they are readily available – and visible.

Emergency exits must be clearly marked and easily accessible.

Bear in mid that depending on the venue you may be required to contact the local authority to check what precautions must be taken to comply with regulations (see Branch 1).

Informing Police

Depending on the number of guests, informing the police is sometimes not only a necessity but an advantage. Forewarned is forearmed, and in my experience if you work with the police with the right attitude they can be extremely helpful. Not so long ago a charming officer even drove a certain guest of mine home – the guest being rather the worse for wear.

On several occasions, instead of towing away badly parked cars they took the trouble to allow us to announce the offending car number so the grateful owner could have the car moved.

FACILITIES & UTILITIES

Parking

When assessing a venue, take parking facilities into account. If you are expecting large numbers of guests to arrive by car, and your party venue does not have adequate parking, you will have to make alternative arrangements. One option is to employ the services of experienced car jockeys (see Branch 8 Staff & Helpers) another is to locate the nearest car park and arrange to have the guests transported to and from the venue.

If a large number of cars are expected do warn neighbouring establishments to help prevent the inconvenience causing bad feelings. I'll never forget my ENGLAND BALL experience. This was the very first Charity Ball which I organized way back in the '70s, to benefit The Council for the Protection of Rural England, at Aubrey House, adjacent to Holland Park London, presided over by the late Lord Henley. A few days before the event the local police informed me I could not proceed with the Ball unless I arranged sufficient car parking facilities. Something I had not anticipated. Fortunately I had an enthusiastic team of voluntary helpers who managed to construct an ingenious wooden bridge and tree walk from the local school playground and car park over the boundary wall. I was lucky the school authorities were helpful, and for me it was a lesson well learned.

Loos/lavatories/bogs/whatever!

Lavatory, WC, bog, the John, head, toilet if you must! Cloakroom, bathroom, washroom, powder room, Men/Women / Ladies/Gents, Little boys room… whatever you wish to call them – they are a must and should be well signed and furnished with ample supplies of necessities, including lavatory paper, soap, tidy bin, tampons, clean hand towels (paper towels are probably more hygienic unless you have a very large supply of small towels and an attendant keeping an eye on things). If the venue does not have sufficient you will need to hire mobile units containing portable chemical lavatories. These can be supplied through the caterers, marquee companies or by checking on the web.

It is also a considerate and good idea to have a selection of safety pins, needle & cotton, hairspray, etc.

Cloakroom

Weather being what it is, and depending on the time of year, it is important to make provision for guests' coats, raincoats, umbrellas, Wellingtons, and even snow boots. If you are entertaining at home, clear a hanging cupboard for this purpose or use a coat rack or hanging rail, which is preferable to a pile of coats, possibly damp or wet dumped on your bed.

If your party is being held elsewhere and the chosen venue have no facilities for coats etc you will need to improvise. The bare necessities are an attendant, dish for tips, coat or hanging rail and ample supplies of hangers and cloakroom tickets.

Hanging rails can be purchased or hired at reasonable cost and are easily dismantled for storing away, as are cheap coat hangers. For cloakroom tickets use raffle tickets, obtainable from stationers.

Power

Check the venue has a sufficient power supply to cope with whatever you may have planned concerning food, drink, and entertainment. Extra power may be needed for bands or discotheque, special effect lighting, heating and air-conditioning equipment.

ACCIDENTS

If accidents occur to guests in your own home, this is generally your responsibility, so check with your insurance to see what is and what is not covered. All commercial establishments should hold public liability insurance, but it never hurts to double check. Whatever the occasion, be prepared for accidents. A first-aid kit is essential. You cannot always count on having a doctor or nurse amongst your guests.

It may be necessary to hire a generator. Most suppliers and entertainers have their own, however you cannot rely on this. So check the power output yourself as overloading the system may, not only be dangerous, but catastrophic if you are suddenly left with no power.

If in doubt ask the professionals.

You will also need to ensure there are sufficient power points and multiple points etc. It is always a good idea to have extra adapters and extension leads handy, just in case.

Air conditioning

Due to the ever-increasing climate changes in today's word, BE PREPARED!

There are the occasional, unexpected heat-waves and being too hot is unpleasant, especially for men in suits or Black Tie. If there is the remote chance that the temperature may soar, make certain you can hire or arrange for portable air-conditioning units or effective fans for the occasion.

Heating

If the venue is a large room, marquee or hall make certain the area has been sufficiently heated before guests arrive and that adequate heating is provided during the event.

If when you first inspect the premises the heating is insufficient, hire industrial heaters for the occasion, so that heat can be blasted where needed, if and when required.

Flooring

The ideal floor for dancing is wood. There is nothing worse than trying to dance on stone or carpet; and grass or sand, although fun, is tiring! If yours is an open-air event or in a marquee then a portable sprung wooden floor will make all the difference and dancing a delight. These can be hired though the marquee, discotheque or entertainment company.

Portable dance floors generally come in 90cm x 90cm sections. They are not expensive and will make a noticeable difference to the enthusiasm that the guests bring to dancing. Indoors, if there are no wooden floorboards to be accessed by

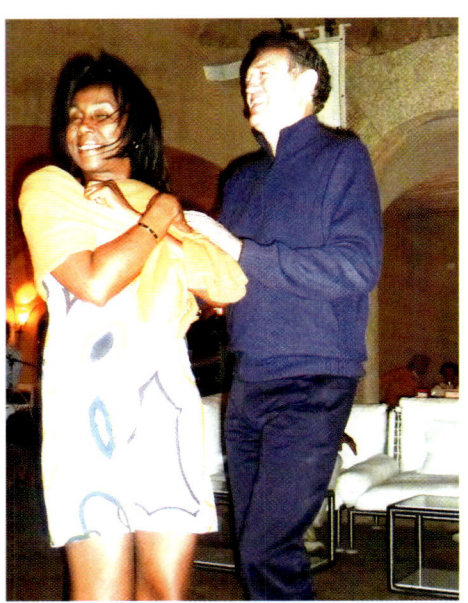

Theresa & Andrew Roberts dancing in Porto Cervo

rolling up the carpet and a portable floor is not possible, then a sheet of cheap linoleum is a possible alternative.

If the venue has an existing dance-floor then the main factor to consider is whether there is sufficient space for entertainment and dancing. Squeezing too many energetic people into a tiny space may be cosy but not much fun and can result in seriously damaged shins!

CATERING CONSIDERATIONS

Whether you decide to self-cater or bring in professionals, the kitchen will be the main focus of work. Hotels and restaurants will have the necessary facilities. However, if you are using a marquee or similar, or if the kitchen is inadequate or too remote from where the action will be taking place, you will need to consider hiring some of the following equipment:

Heating units, hot plates, portable ovens, or even a mobile kitchen.

Also, if you don't anticipate using cold-storage units, you will need to allocate a small room or protected cool area that can be used for storing freshly prepared food. You may also need to set up a dispense bar.

All these factors, which incur additional expense, should be taken into account when assessing the cost of using the venue.

Be bold
Be brave...

branch 4

décor and theme

Effective décor sets the mood of the party as soon as the guests arrive, igniting their enthusiasm and leaving a lasting impression. Therefore give the theme and décor careful thought and time.

The usual tools are lighting, flowers & greenery, however a total transformation will depend on your budget.

You may even want to bring in the professionals, who obviously have at their disposal a great variety of ideas and the necessary props to realize your dream theme.

This has become a competitive market and so it is worth gaining a few quotes and suggestions before making any decisions.

If expense is a consideration then rely on your own enthusiasm, energy, and sense of creativity.

When strapped for cash and searching for inspiration and props I have struck lucky with local interior designers offering me bales of discarded fabric, local theatres who have let me loose in their prop archives, and kind stores who have on occasions lent me an Aladdin's cave worth of window and display materia . I have

A colourful way to serve canapés

even found art colleges with creative students willing to help put their talents to the test. When you put your mind to it you will find there are no end of opportunities to beg, borrow or barter.

HELP WITH DÉCOR

If you are not bringing in the professionals, then help is a must.

Put together an enthusiastic team of helpers, whether your friends, your kids, their friends, or whoever, it will surprise you how people love to be involved. Remember though, to give credit where credit is due. People, naturally need to feel appreciated and sometimes in the hustle, bustle, thrill and speed of things we overlook people's feelings. With voluntary and unpaid helpers especially, make certain you notice their input, show your appreciation, and mean it.

In the past I have been fortunate, when organising Charity events, to have had an eager team of serving officers from one of Her Majesty's Regiments to help blow up my balloons. I also found them brilliant for heralding in a special guest, the cake, announcing dinner, or a speaker. On one occasion their reward was to meet the legendary star, Dame Shirley Bassey. They were naturally thrilled — as was the Dame!

Dame Shirley Bassey flanked by two trumpeters

FLORAL DECORATION

Nothing beats the pure simplicity and effect of carefully selected and exquisitely arranged freshly cut flowers. Today there is so much talent and expertise within this field that it has emerged as a complete art form. I have seen and indeed achieved impressive displays using everything from cabbages to bales of hay.

Herewith are a few ideas:

- Spiders webs woven simply from wool or thread spanning white, silver or gold-sprayed branches of trees

- Fruit, vegetables and leaves, threaded securely with wire and wound around tent poles to disguise the poles

- Cascades of trailing greenery and pure-white flowers smothering balconies and banisters to give a breath-taking romantic effect

- Entwining flowers and greenery around tables, chair backs, doors and windows

- Spraying leaves, nuts, fruit, dried flowers and twigs with silver, gold or coloured paint to match a theme then wiring them in with the foliage. Leaves, especially, can be most effective when sprayed the colour of your theme and used profusely as camouflage or scattered over the tablecloth

- 30cm. inflated multi-coloured metallic jester masks, with flowing streams of assorted cheap florist ribbons. Intertwined with trailing bunches of greenery and wired together with fairy lights strung around the sides of the walls, or marquee and tent poles

Whether real or fake, flowers are enormously worthwhile. Mixing real and faux is an art, but satisfactory results are not difficult to achieve.

Flower Markets

Visiting the flower markets in the early hours of the morning is an exhilarating experience and well worth the effort. Apart from the sight and smell of all the fresh trees, plants and flowers, the atmosphere and jollity of the buyers and traders even at 4am is infectious. At London's New Covent Garden Market, Nine Elms, south of the Thames, there is an intriguing cross-section of early risers, from Ivana Trump, personally selecting her favourite orchids and white lilies having arrived direct from the airport on route to her London apartment to various specialists in flora decor.

To buy from the Flower Market you need to:

- Get up early!
- Pay a small entrance fee as you drive in
- Have a suitable vehicle in which to carry your purchases

Table extravaganza created by
Rob van Heldon for
Terence Cole's birthday in Capri

Apple display,
The Club at the Ivy, London

Florists' Materials

Creating powerful and spectacular floral displays is made easier if you use the proper tools and accessories now available and easy to purchase at the flower markets.

In addition to ribbon, wire and assorted foam-block bases for wet or dry arrangements (invaluable for table centres), there are numerous items that can help achieve the desired result.

At Nine Elms Flower Market, London, these suppliers are situated at the four corners of the Market and supply every imaginable accessory to creating table centres displays and décor for every occasion for significant and important celebrations, including birthday's weddings, babies, Valentines, Halloween, Thanksgiving, St Patrick's Day, Christmas, New Year Hanukkah & Yom Kippur.

Faking your foliage

Years ago when I lived in Portugal's Algarve in what was a tiny fishing village called Albufeira and discovered I did not possess green fingers I planted my entire cliff top garden with plastic flowers. Things were very basic in those days! It caused quite an alarm amongst the locals and a huge amount of amusement to the ever-flowing number of guests who passed through my house. There has been significant progress since then and fake is no longer frowned upon. In fact the selection is so vast and real in many cases, you'll never know, unless you touch.

Even artificial grass, is so realistic, it's almost impossible to know the difference.

ICE

Ice Sculpture

Ice Sculpture is effective and fun and specialist ice cutters and even chefs perform miracles. Bespoke shapes though, take time to produce and as an art form they don't come cheap. However, popular moulds are available and thus sculptures can be easily and economically produced to order.

Incidentally remember that the ice melts and space for drip trays, supplied, must be taken into consideration when placing the sculptures.

PRINTED BALLOONS

Consider printing balloons with a message or appropriate wording. Alternatively do it yourself and use a thick felt tip pen. This attention to details is fun and guests generally take them away.

Dry-ice or fog machines

These machines are available for hire and effective for creating a misty effect when guests arrive, during Cabaret, bringing in a cake etc. Do, however, take into consideration that the dry ice which generates the effect, is in fact solid carbon dioxide, so it goes without saying that these machines need careful supervision and are not overused, especially indoors, as it could cause a reaction and irritation of mucous membranes such as the eyes and the respiratory tract associated with extended exposure.

BALLOONS

Balloons continue to add that particular party magic to an occasion with so many different types, sizes and colours. The only chore involved — once you have made your selection is getting them inflated, tied, grouped, and positioned.

Their impact value resides primarily in quantity: the more you use — the greater the effect. As impact is the goal don't scrimp on numbers. If for budget reasons you decide not to use the services of a balloon company, you can hire a gas cylinder and have at least a few patient helpers to deal with this exercise. Balloons take careful planning, as fully inflated their life is limited. If they are to remain looking fresh, inflating should be done five or six hours before the event and as near as possible to the location, especially when creating large clusters.

If you plan to place the balloons outside, keep them out of direct sunlight. Balloons perish quickly in the sun; so to prolong their appearance, position them in the shade until needed.

Entrance or party indicators

Bunches of balloons are helpful to indicate the entrance to an event and are an instant sign of the party's location. However make certain to have security on the door as they can also act as an open invitation to potential gatecrashers and undesirables.

Burlesque waitress at Tallulah Rendall's Album launch with balloons

Balloon sculpture

This is a proven way of creating an impact and balloon sculptures I have used, have included life-sized soldiers, guarding an entrance; arches leading to dance floors, numerous celebratory messages, Mickey Mouse and Donald Duck and even a life-sized Harley Davidson bike with rider – all formed from combining a mass of balloons. This requires real skill and a great deal of patience and therefore usually needs a professional creative hand.

Balloons within balloons

The creation of a balloon or balloons within a balloon is very popular nowadays. These can be ordered over the Internet.

Balloon lights

Illuminate your balloons with slow/fast/super fast or stay on balloon LED lights.

Netted for release

Balloons in a fine net, (available from a fishing tackle shop) loosely secured and suspended from a high point or the ceiling is an effective way of creating a buzz when released at the appropriate moment freeing the balloons to float down over the guests and dance floor.

LIGHTING

The following are creative lighting possibilities. This is simply a selection of possibilities, which can be found on line, and hired or put together yourself.

- Fairy lights
- Skytracker search lights
- Flood lighting
- Illuminated dance floors
- Silk flame lights
- Torches and flares
- Candles – real & battery operated
- Nightlights
- Candle holders
- Glow and flashing sticks/accessories
- Fibre optic
- String or rope lights
- Solar lanterns
- Under table skirt lights
- Crystal light up ice cubes
- Lighted shot glasses

Rupert Appleyard's Balloon Bike at Flemings Hotel Mayfair

The entertainers welcoming guests arriving at
Dame Shirley's 70th Birthday party at Cliveden

If working to a strict budget then consider the following suggestions:

Fairy lights

Simple fairy lights add a romantic magical effect especially when used in large quantities and twined around branches or added to the general décor. Extension leads are a necessity.

Flares

Flares up a drive, placed around the grounds or lining a path add a dramatic effect. Generally sold in boxes of fifty they are available from garden centres or the barbecue section of department stores. Depending on the effect you wish to achieve, a good guide would be to place them about 2 to 3 metres apart. The average flare lasts approximately three hours.

One of several marquees created by Mona Al-Khatib for an Indian themed evening garden party in her garden at Wentworth for a significant Birthday

Liz and Mona Al-Khatib dressed with 'A touch of the Raj'

Candles

Candles are best purchased in bulk, either from a good discount outlet or from the flower market, but make certain you buy long-lasting non-drip candles. It is worth paying a little more as they will go much further and not make a mess. When placing candles take care to ensure that they will not become fire hazards, so make certain they are firmly fixed into their holders.

Nightlights

Nightlights induce a twinkling glowing effect but as they are fiddly to light, the easiest solution is to use a battery operated flame ignition lighter. When I entertain at home I place them outside my front door and up each side of my steps as a welcome approach to guests and set the tone for what may be to follow. So long as they are placed within small glass containers they will burn for hours and can safely be placed around a garden, balcony, on window ledges or on surfaces around a room. If you wish you could add a few drops from an old bottle of fragrance to the nightlights to enhance the air. Don't overdo it though; all the guests may have an allergic reaction!

Candle holders

Virtually any appropriately sized container can be adapted to hold candles. Important points to remember are:

Candles must be securely gripped or fixed to their holder and in addition to melting the base of the candle I find using a reusable adhesive such as Blue Tac most effective.

To ensure there is something to collect any dripping wax.

There are special candleholders for flower arrangements; designed to be used in conjunction with florists' foam blocks or Oasis, but frankly pushing the candle directly and firmly into the blocks is usually sufficient.

DEVELOPING A THEME

Enjoy the process of developing the theme from the moment you 'dream your event' as each stage is a significant step. Starting with the invitations, bear in mind, this is the first visible sign of your celebration and the time to impress, stimulate, and ignite the imagination of your selected guests.

Follow the theme through to tie in with your décor, food, dress, and indeed the total look of the event. You may find guests surprise you and take things a few steps further. I remember one such occasion when I had chosen an Adam & Eve theme… I leave the rest to your imagination!

A cleverly thought out original theme creates an impressive and memorable atmosphere and the result is fun for all concerned. It also gives people a good opportunity to add their own particular touch of creativity to the occasion. It is of course, in addition, a brilliant ice-breaker!

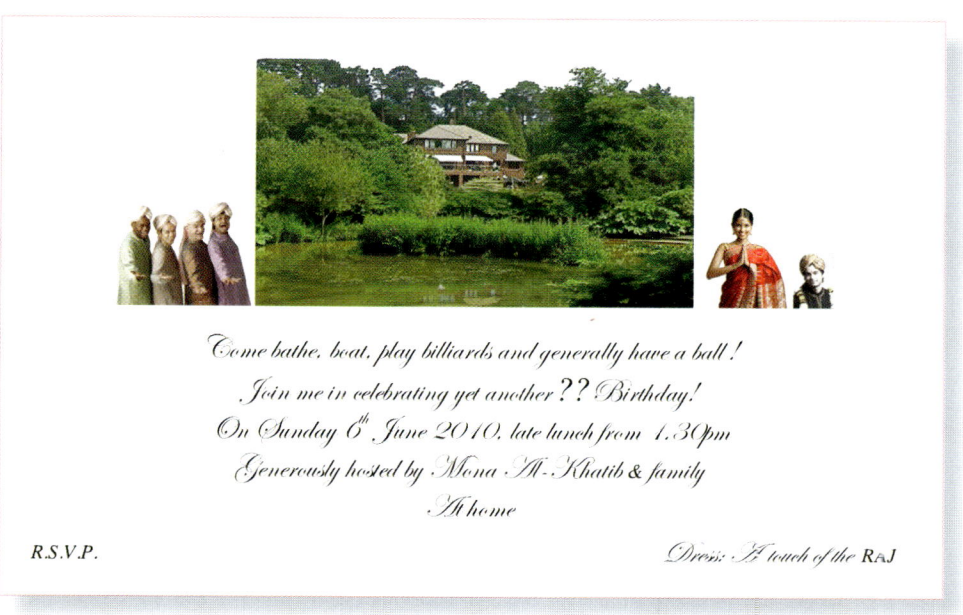

Come bathe, boat, play billiards and generally have a ball!
Join me in celebrating yet another ?? Birthday!
On Sunday 6th June 2010, late lunch from 1.30pm
Generously hosted by Mona Al-Khatib & family
At home

R.S.V.P.   *Dress: A touch of the Raj*

A 'Touch of the Raj' Invitation. The address and RSVP information has been deliberately removed

When possible match your theme to the reason for the event. Consider something either totally over the top and adventurous, or straight forward and simple. A party I remember with significance, was one which friends gave to celebrate their wedding at London's Roundhouse in Camden with an exotic jungle theme. However what caused the biggest stir was receiving the hand-delivered invitation in an impressive wooden box, which had to be opened personally when delivered: once opened out flew two butterflies, revealing the invitation nestling amongst a few fake butterflies After such an invitation it was obvious things could only get more extravagant – which they certainly did!

One of the first televised Charity events I organised was a 'Prize Guys Celebrity Auction', which raised funds for some leading cancer charities, attended by 300 of London's most glamorous and successful female dynamos. A male celebrity was packaged with a tempting auction lot and sold to the highest female bidder. The production company at that time, Action Time, and the programme had been commissioned by ITV.

The occasion had a theme of decadence, heavy glamour, and romance. To enhance this I had ordered 200, helium filled, gold and blue metallic balloons in the shape of celestial suns and moons. These were possibly the first of this type and therefore that alone caused quite a stir. The balloons swirled above the heads of this attractive scene which was embellished with the addition of two gold-sprayed actors portraying the gods Bacchus and Apollo.

'Costume' or 'Fancy dress' as referred to in the UK

Apart from adding to the colourful ambience of the occasion and another effective proven 'ice-breaker', the real plus with Costume, Masquerade, or Fancy Dress is the opportunity it provides for invitees to cast off their inhibitions and often, take on the actual character being portrayed! I once dressed appropriately with seven veils, for a '1001 Nights' birthday celebration, and still remember the fun I had when not a soul recognised me, the flirtatious character behind the yashmak.

Costumes don't necessarily need to be hired, although this is the easy solution. Far more fun is gained from creating your own and it is amazing what can be accomplished, once you use your imagination.

At a masked ball held at London's Royal Albert Hall, the famous 1970s tailor Tom Gilbey turned up wearing dark glasses, a gondolier's hat with his head stuck through the slats of a large blind. What was he? Of course, a 'Venetian blind!' Controversial maybe, but an inventive, clever concoction and years later still memorable.

At one of the last century's significant birthday parties, hosted by Lord & Lady Montagu at their stately home Beaulieu, guests were invited to come dressed to the

House of Lords and Vivienne Westwood's model being greeted by Sir James Cayzer, Mark Law & Aline Hay of Duns

theme, 'if music be the food of love – play on'. A challenge? Not, it seemed for the few hundred guests who attended including myself, transformed as SHEET MUSIC, dressed in two short white sheets back and front, adorned with black musical notes cut from electrical sticky tape. Simple and yet it shows what can be achieved with a little focused imagination and a few props.

Masks & props

There are always guests who are reticent in taking costume or theme parties seriously, perhaps not having the courage to participate. So for fear of looking silly or being the only one, they play safe. If on arrival they then discover most guests have made a real effort and they are in the minority, they can feel somewhat left out and now really stand apart regretting not being more adventurous.

A well-prepared host should have a supply of assorted masks, scarves, hats, inventive headgear, cheap jewellery or whatever appropriate available to offer guests who couldn't be bothered or were reluctant to take the theme/costume dress code seriously. Including a supply of theatrical make-up, and even a professional make-up artist or face-painter is also an excellent idea.

Professional face painting is an intriguing and always a popular attraction to a party. Face painters can transform the entire face into a spectacular animal likeness or paint motifs, including flowers or intricate patterns with jewels etc as well as theatrical make-up.

Exotic non-permanent body art of the East is also fun as is henna painting which takes about fifteen minute per guest with the work mainly done on hands, arms or around the belly button.

Henna is in fact a plant, and has been used in both the Middle East and India for thousands of years to create beautiful, temporary skin art. Applied to the skin, it stains through the outer layer leaving marks, which last until worn off. Henna can also be used to colour hair and create an exotic red tone.

Musical toys/instruments

If you wish to include a musical ingredient to your party and want to encourage guests to join in the spirit of the occasion – especially during the dancing – supply an assortment of simple musical instruments. Toy tambourines, drums, mouth organs,

Lucinda Watson's 18th '1001 Nights' Birthday party at Kits Club London

Dancers at Lucinda Watson's party at Kits Club London

75

Aladdin's Cave with an
assortment of props, which I
created for Lucinda Watson's
'1001 Nights' Birthday Party

and accordions can be fun as of course the Mexican or Brazilian maracas. Ethnic shops generally have an assortment of rattles, simple drums, and hand-carved whistles – all most effective and inexpensive.

In Bali, at a New Year's Eve party I attended as a guest of my sister, Victoria Watson, and her husband Ian, with my niece Lucinda and my daughter Talulah Rendall we were each given a simple bamboo rattle, available in the local markets for a few cents. This single rattle, called the Angklung, is part of the Balinese Angklung Gamelan ensemble of instruments, which are played at all the traditional dances, religious festivals and ceremonies in Bali. Each rattle is tuned according to its number, so:

1 = doh, 2 = ray, 3 = me, 4 = fa, 5 = so, 6 = lah, 7 = te, and 8 = doh

The conductor instructed us to rattle our instruments in time with the numbers displayed on a large board. After a few attempts we mastered the rattles and, with 100 or so other participants, successfully play 'Auld Lang Syne' to perfection at midnight.

Angklung

'After a good dinner one can forgive anybody, even one's own relations'

OSCAR WILDE

A Woman of No Importance

branch 5

the table

TABLE SIZE

Table size will be determined not purely by your choice, but often by the size and shape of the location. Circular tables, seating six, eight, ten or twelve may be perfect for one shape of room; whereas a series of trestle tables could be the ideal solution for another.

If you lack the necessary serving tables, trestle tables, or the collapsible picnic variety are suitable alternatives.

FLOOR PLAN

The way to determine your requirements is to make a floor plan. Then using cut outs shapes of the tables and chairs, play around until you find the right layout for the number of guests. With the necessary software, this can be done on a computer.

TABLE LINEN / TABLECLOTHS

Tablecloths

Most colours, shapes, and size of tablecloths and napkins can be hired. Select colour, size, and style and agree a price.

Old sheets

If for whatever reason you decide not to hire, old sheets could be used as a base, spread over a silence cloth, if necessary, made from felt or some other suitable alternative.

Ideally, the sheet will cover the table legs to the floor, which is useful when joining a mishmash of unmatched tables of different sizes together or indeed to add conformity to a number of tables. Smaller sheets or lengths of cloth could also be tacked together and cut to size, allowing at least an inch to flow onto the floor.

These underclothes (sheets) can be hidden by smaller over cloths, which cover the tops of the tables, in the fabric of your choice in keeping with your theme or the mood you wish to create: theatrical, rustic, dramatic, elegant, humorous – whatever. These can be cut from cheap material such as lining material, satin, mattress ticking, sacking or nylon net, which is available from department stores in many, different vibrant colours including gold, silver.

Fireproof

When ordering fabric remember, to check whether it is, or needs to be, treated to make it fireproof.

Professional effect

For a more formal, professional effect, use a cloth large enough to cover the table top of each table. Then use a separate length of cloth, with the width equal to the height of the table (top to floor) and pin or slip stitch it around the edge of the table, making small pleats every few inches. If you feel the necessity to cover the joins – swathes of fabric, broad ribbons, or trailing leaves are ideal.

The Banqueting look. Length of fabric pinned around the table

Designing your own pattern

With a little time and thought you can include your linen in the theme. Experiment with potato cuts, wooden or rubber dye stamps, spray paints, or even coloured glues that expand, glow, and glitter when dry.

Table Napkins

Napkins are primarily for protecting your clothes and wiping your mouth and fingers.

Paper napkins ought to be kept for picnics, children's parties, outdoor entertaining, and cocktail parties.

Formal dining requires fabric or superior quality paper napkins, which can have logo or personal message printed etc.

If you are following a theme through to the linen, then you could either buy inexpensive napkins in bulk from a wholesalers or chain store and add your own design, or, as I once did when my budget was miniscule, launder and starch some old cotton sheets, and cut them into suitably sized squares. Hemming is unnecessary and they look particularly stylish tied with strands of raffia, ribbon, or string.

Napkins folded or napkin holders

This is a matter of personal choice. Frankly I am not a fan of fancy folded napkins – probably the result of having frequented too many hotel restaurants. My preference is for a simply tied or carefully folded napkin.

If you are into the origami type of folded napkins there is a very good folding guide on the web.

At a series of 'Breakfast At Tiffany's' Champagne breakfast I hosted some years ago at Tiffany's in Old Bond Street, a bracelet of precious jewels secured the table napkin of each of my guests. They had huge fun comparing the price tags, which ranged from £5,000 to £150,000. Needless to say the napkin holders were NOT allowed out of the dining room!

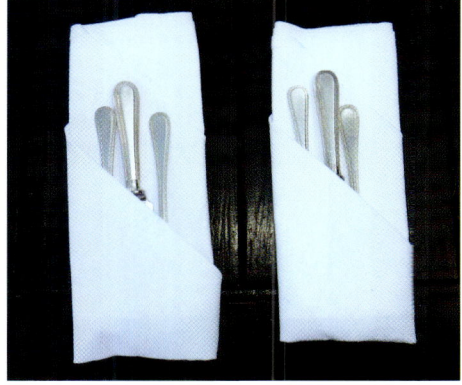

Table napkins suitable for buffet or informal dining

TABLE MATS

Tablemats are for the purpose of decoration or protecting a good quality tabletop. The size is up to individual taste and should relate to the amount of room allocated to each guest.

If small mats are used, the cutlery can be placed either side of the mat rather than on it.

Mats are fun to include in the theme, especially if they are visible and not covered by the first course. I have occasionally had mats created specially from a photograph relating to the event. Inevitably the guests will take them, as a memento of the occasion.

Should you wish to do this yourself, you can create a customized placemat out of scanned photographs. Simply print to the appropriate size and either have them professionally laminated in plastic or do it yourself with a laminating machine.

TABLE DECORATIONS

When selecting table decorations it is important to bear in mind, people need to see and be seen.

The golden rule is: keep table centres and decorations lower or higher than eye contact height.

Impressive table decorations can be obtained with minimum effort but they nevertheless require a fair amount of forethought and attention. Think theatrically – First impression is all-important to an occasion and an exquisitely and imaginatively decorated table will create a lasting sensation – as will the photographs!

Consider space and bear in mind the amount of room available on the tabletop. Above all be practical. Once the table is laid with plates, cutlery, table napkins, glasses, name cards, salt and pepper, menus, water and wine etc., space will be at a premium. Therefore, It is best to concentrate the main part of the decoration along or in the centre of the table.

A fun festive over-cloth I have demonstrated a couple of times on TV was created from a length of gold net with little bells, available from most haberdasheries, sewn or attached with safety pins every few inches around the edge.

Table setting surrounding Alex Cole at another party created by Rob Van Helden for Terence & Niki Cole in Capri

Table Centres

The style of the table centre depends on the shape and length of the table.

Long or oval tables require long low trailing foliage, flowers and whatever other accessories you choose. Sometimes the table requires more than one centrepiece. A good guide is to allow a centrepiece every third or fourth person. If you like you can fill in the empty gaps by extending greenery between each arrangement. This can look very effective especially if intertwined with candles and nightlights.

For large round or square tables, height gives impact but this should be achieved without blocking the view of guests. This can be done in various ways but, as in all things, there are fashion vogues with flower arrangements so either be original or follow whatever is the latest trend.

Candelabra

Classic silver candelabra are always elegant and a romantic form of table lighting. These can be hired and many establishments supply them automatically.

There are inexpensive plastic versions, available from party shops and flower markets. If you consider using these then I would suggest you camouflage them dramatically with greenery, flowers, or ribbon so that only a glimpse of silver twinkles through. A few strands of trailing slim pliable branches should work effectively and you can always wire a few flowers etc around the stems to give an even more professional touch. Unless you are in a minimalist mood – think drama and go with the flow.

PLACE CARDS

Once you have compiled the names of all guests attending, you can either start writing by hand or printing their names on place cards. Whether or not you use their full name and title will depend on the tone and formality of the occasion. The important point is to ensure that you are consistent: do not write Mrs John Smith on one place card and Joan Smith or even Joan on the other.

Titled guests should be styled socially, i.e. Lord Snooks, not The Earl of Snooks.

Stationers and printers have cards specifically for this purpose, however these cards are not difficult to make and can be done easily on a computer. You could also simply cut your own from sheets of quality paper or card. Using a paper/card cutter would make this easier.

In the past I have used the following alternatives with success:

- Toy tin soldiers carrying the guest's name on a small slip of card
- Fresh leaves with the name written bolding in gold or silver
- Torn brown paper, tucked into the napkin tie with the guest's name
- Menu Cards with the guest's name handwritten on the top
- Gas-filled balloons with each guest's name handwritten using a felt-tip pen attached to the back of the individual's chair using long strands of ribbon

Remember at this stage to have an ample supply of extra place cards or whatever you have chosen for this purpose, as numerous changes occur with your guest list between the time guests accept and the time they actually arrive.

Calligraphy

Sadly a dying art, however the effect of hand-written calligraphy is impressive and shows great style, so, if you decide to stick to using conventional place cards but think your handwriting is not up to scratch, find a good calligrapher to assist you. They normally charge according to the number of names required. Alternatively you can do it on your printer.

MENU CARDS

Menu cards are another personal touch, showing a degree of thought and attention to detail. Once the menu is decided these can either be printed on the computer or carefully handwritten by you, your helpers, (should you be lucky enough to have any) or an expert calligrapher.

With any important occasion the menu card is an ideal place to state the name of the host or hosts, the date and the reason for the celebration, as some guests like to keep the menu card as a record of the occasion.

You may also wish to add details of the wine and whether there will be any speeches and if so by whom.

I have been fortunate to have attended three dinners at Buckingham Palace and one at Highgrove the home of Their Royal Highnesses The Prince of Wales and The Duchess of Cornwall and have always been so impressed with the artistically created menus showing originality and great style

TABLE GIFTS

However small or insignificant, an attractively wrapped table gift is a touching and charming way of welcoming guests to the table. Regardless of the content, they will be gratefully received and, I can assure you taken home and kept. I have seen many 'superstars' seriously upset at the end of the evening upon discovering that their wee gift had 'walked'!

As to the choice of gift, there are so many new products continually competing for attention especially in the cosmetic and fragrance world, so it is worth contacting the company PRs to see if they have any special promotions planned. In which case they may be only too willing to give you sufficient samples for your guests.

Small musical instruments are always popular as gifts in addition to being an ideal way of encouraging your guests to participate.

A buttonhole for the men and corsage for the women is another charming idea, although, in today's world considered somewhat quaint.

Buckingham Palace menu cards

TABLE PLAN

The secret weapon of successful hosting.

It is the host's prerogative to decide the seating plan. After all, you do know your guests (or at least most of them) and likely to know their preferences. So treat this challenge with the right attitude and you will find it fascinating and although occasionally challenging, rather like doing a large puzzle. I have to admit I thoroughly enjoy this part of the planning.

The easiest way to tackle this task is to first sort the place cards with the guest's names into alphabetical order. If, as I have already advised, you have kept your list of attendees in this order, this will not be difficult.

Then sort the names into groups representing tables, arranging them so that each table will have someone who you feel will hold the table together. Thoroughly mix, match and swap around the names until you can almost hear the conversation, which could take place. This done then mark the reverse of each place card with the number of the table and the seat e.g. Table 1 seat 1. If you feel confident enough in your selection you could even by-pass this stage and merely stack the place cards in the order of your proposed seating for each table and place a rubber band around each pile of place cards.

Table Numbers or Names

If there are more that three or four tables then table numbers or table names are necessary in order to help people locate their table.

Your caterer or banqueting manager at the venue will normally supply table numbers on request, but if not, then providing your own is an easy task. You can either make them yourself or buy them ready made to slot into holders or stick into the table centres.

Table names are a fun alternative to numbers especially with a theme. For example, if your theme is 'CARNIVAL' then table names could be: Clowns, Mardi Gras, Masks, Musicians, or whatever to fit the theme. The centrepiece of each table could be in keeping with the name, for example the Masks table could sport an assortment of crazy Venetian carnival masks.

A former Turkish Ambassador's wife used to host splendid dinner parties for around a hundred guests. When you arrived and entered the main drawing room for drinks before dinner, each guest had to pick a card from one of two baskets. One basket with a pink bow was for women, and the other with a blue bow for men. Each card had an illustration of, or was attached to a flower. When it was time to be seated for dinner you had to find the table whose centre piece was a display of the flower on your place card – a very clever idea, saving a great deal of time and effort with arranging precise placements, but of course you had no control over who sat next to whom.

GUESTS CHANGING PLACE CARDS

Golden Rule for guests concerning Place cards is NEVER re-arrange the seating plan. This is a cardinal sin and to peek at the table settings before dinner and swap the place cards around is not only annoying for the host, who presumably has deliberately sorted out the placement according to their liking, but can be very embarrassing for the culprit if caught out! It a guest has a problem with the seating he or she should quietly explain to the host and let the host rectify the situation.

CHAIRS

I get so frustrated with continually having to sit on banqueting or even normal chairs, which are far too low for the table. You end up virtually resting your chin on the table!

Fed up with asking for a cushion as this happens so often, I always take a shawl with me to sit on, in order to be at the right height.

So if you are hiring chairs, check they are a suitable height for your tables.

Design and condition of chairs is all too often overlooked and yet they do much to enhance or detract from the overall setting: the sight of a beautifully laid dining room whether for six, twenty, a hundred or even a thousand guests, is so easily marred by unsightly chairs. Depending on the supplier's selection and your budget, chairs could be wooden, plastic, small gold banqueting, foldaway or stackable, with or without armrests.

If you are working within a tight budget and consider the assortment of chairs you have available are unappealing, be they hired, or simply dining, kitchen, garden, or whatever, the solution is to disguise them with covers – even the cheapest plastic variety can be transformed into 'Cinderellas for the night.'

Whether you hire chair covers through caterers (sensible for large numbers) or, for almost the same cost but more effort, you choose to do it yourself the transformation is worth the cost or time involved.

LAYING THE TABLE

Past generations have drawn up numerous rules for entertaining especially when dining in great style, when an abundance of staff was the norm and a way of life. Today the approach to laying tables is more relaxed, although this does not mean that your table should be laid in a slapdash or an inelegant manner.

Unless of course, the theme of your party happens to be 'Bad Taste'.

Normally the quality and choice of cutlery, glassware, and crockery/china is relative to your budget, quality of caterer or chosen venue. If you wish to inject your own style, especially when dealing with low numbers, then this is an area where you can be creative, resourceful and show flair.

COVERING A PARTY CHAIR

Lay a length of cloth over the chair and secure with a large bow, tied at seat or back level at the rear. If the chair has arms, more fabric will be required and slits made through the sides of the fabric at the corners of the rear base of the seat to thread ties around to the back in order to keep the fabric in place.

Sashes over chair covers at the venue, Altitude, at the top of Millbank Tower, London.

Impressive table setting
on board
Terence & Niki Cole's yacht

When entertaining small numbers, never worry about not having sufficient settings of your best dinner service or knives and forks. There is nothing wrong with mixing different styles and patterns.

Frequently I have:

- Arranged each place setting with a different style of china, cutlery and glasses
- Used two styles of everything, alternating the place settings
- Organized a seated dinner at home for twelve using the place settings of a dozen different well-known London restaurants (supplied I might add from the owners)
- Purchased an entire plain white reject dinner service and range of glasses. I then painted the plates in keeping with my theme, which was a 21st Birthday celebration, and wrote the name of each guest on the glasses, with painting pens
- Simply borrowed!

The equipment and utensils need to suit the food and drink being offered.

When deciding on appropriate crockery and cutlery consider your menu and write down each course, remember to include what may also be needed for a reception. If canapés are being offered these will require serving dishes or trays.

The following list is a guide to what could be required, however, if in doubt, ask! There are many people around delighted to help – including the manager of a local restaurant, or banqueting manager of a venue or catering company.

Depending on your order, occasionally the wine merchant supplying the drink – spirits, wines, soft drinks, sodas and ice etc., will include the glasses on a complimentary basis. However, remember when hiring or borrowing glasses and other items to keep the container boxes in a convenient place and check whether the items need to be clean before they are returned.

Michael & Sophie Hanna's Bad Taste Invitation

equipment and utensils

This is a selection, which could be a guide when choosing your particular requirements.

CUTLERY

First course: small fork, or small knife & fork
Soup: Soup spoon.
Main course: Large knife & fork. Sharp knife if game or steak is to be served
Salad: Small fork.
Cheese: Small knife.
Pudding: desert or pudding spoon and fork. Teaspoon.
Coffee or tea: Teaspoon.
Butter: Small knife.

Rudi Jagersbacher about to enjoy some beluga caviar!

CAVIAR

Requires either small mother of pearl or bone spoons, or a small fork if served with blinis. (or if blinis are not available, small crackers or tiny pieces of lightly toasted brown bread). Believe it or not, the correct way of eating caviar is licking the Beads off the top of your left wrist!

Serving caviar is best presented in the actual tin or placed on a glass bowl resting, on a bed of crushed ice, within another large bowl.

Some hosts may think serving caviar with eggs or sour cream appropriate; this is incorrect, as these additional flavourings will only change the taste of the caviar.

If, however the caviar used, is of a lesser quality, then sour cream, chopped white and yoke of hardboiled eggs, chives & onion may help to disguise this fact.

CROCKERY

Bread: Small side plate.
First course: Medium size plate or smaller as appropriate
Soup: Soup bowl with or without handles, or suitable cup.
Main course: Large Plate – round, square or oblong – your choice.
Salad: Side dish or small plate.
Pudding:Dish/bowl or suitable container.
Cheese:Small Plate.
Fruit: Suitable dish.
Coffee/tea: Cup and saucer.
Milk/cream jug. Sugar bowl.
Miscellaneous: Finger bowl, if fingers have been used during any course.
e.g. corn on the cob, shellfish, etc.
Celery holder, usually glass (similar to a flower vase), if served during cheese.

SERVING DISHES

These need to be large enough to contain the food and light enough to be either carried or passed around the table. Lids help to contain the heat but best to remove during serving, as they can be cumbersome.

GLASSWARE

ON GUEST'S ARRIVAL:

Champagne, wine, cocktail, spirit or water glasses, depending on what is being served.

DURING A MEAL:

Shot glass if serving vodka (with caviar) or whisky (with haggis perhaps?)
Small wine glass for white wine
Larger wine glass for red wine (thus allowing the wine ample room to breath)
Water Glass
Small or very small glass for Port or Liqueur.
Brandy Glass

Tips concerning wine glasses

Glasses for wine need to be large enough to allow swirling, as this helps release the flavour of the wine.

Brandy glasses should have an inward-curved rim to enhance the heady bouquet, therefore, use a glass, which is as large as possible but serve no more than 60 grams (2 oz).

Cognac, a type of brandy, needs a smaller type of balloon glass, as connoisseurs believe the larger brandy glass allows the cognac's bouquet to escape the glass too quickly.

Port needs to show off its aroma and colour and therefore should not be poured more than halfway into the glass.

The tradition of passing the Port to the left

This tradition of serving Port is believed to come from the British navy. The decanter of port is placed in front of the host who then serves the guest to his right, the host then passes the decanter to the guest on his left (port-side). The port is then passed to the left all the way back to the host.

DECANTER

Anyone who wants the best from their wine should own a decanter and although most wines on the shelves today have no real need for decanting, many still benefit. This should be done at least one hour before drinking.

Good wine

especially red, which may have aged in bottle, will throw sediment. This is displeasing to the eye and can be quite unpleasant in the mouth.

Young wine

also can benefit from decanting, although the aim is not to take the wine off its sediment (there is rarely any) but rather to aerate the wine in order to soften its youthful bite and encourage the development of the more complex aromas.

So, if the first taste of your preferred wine reveals a tannic, grippy, structure, decanting can really help.

Decantering aged wines

If the bottle of wine you plan to serve has been previously stored horizontally in a wine cellar, first let the bottle stand up for at least two hours. This helps any sediment settle to the bottom.

Next, hold up the bottle to a lamp or candle in order to pinpoint the areas in which sediment has formed.

Uncork the wine, and pour very slowly into the decanter, taking care to avoid any sediment. If you see sediment in the bottle's neck, cease pouring. The last third of the bottle is more likely to contain sediment, so pay careful attention during this part of the pour. LEAVE the last portion, approximately half a cup in the bottle.

If the wine had been bottled for an extended period of time, it will require more time to release flavours into the air so for maximum results, decant the wine at least an hour before drinking, but NEVER MORE THAN EIGHT, as it will oxidize and the flavour will taste acidic like vinegar.

A CONVENTIONAL PLACE SETTING

The following section's guide to laying a table will make life easier for the host, those serving, and for those enjoying the meal. However as I frequently point out, there is no-one up there, telling us guys down here,

"Thou shall not stray from conventional guidelines"

There is nothing wrong with using a standard wine glass throughout a meal, and if you wish to serve your salad on a palm leaf on a bed of ice on a saucer, or your fish 'n' chips in paper – so be it!

Food needs to look inviting and so long as the preparation and presentation are scrupulously hygienic you can be inventive.

Cutlery

Once the cutlery is selected, according to your menu, start laying it in the order in which it will be used, working from the outside towards the plate for each course served. So the first course cutlery will be placed farthest from the plate and so on and so forth. It is wise not to vary this, as most guests will know to start from the outside and work in.

The knives & forks should be placed at right angles and approximately 20 centimetres from the edge of the table, to reduce the risk of them falling onto the floor.

Knives should have their cutting edge towards the plate and in UK the fork tines are usually turned upwards, except it would appear in smart Italian restaurants!

The butter knife can be placed either across the bread plate, or on the right of the place setting.

If soup is being served, place the soupspoon to the right of the large knife.

Pudding fork and spoon are generally placed above the place setting, or 'cover' as it is occasionally referred, parallel to each other with the spoon above, facing to the right. More formally these can be treated in the same way as the other cutlery and placed either side of the cover. (spoon on the right, fork on the left), inside the main cutlery.

At one time different types of forks were used for different types of food. E.g. the fork used for hors d'oeuvres was different to those used for fish, meat, salad or pudding. Today the difference is generally in size not style. Fish knives and forks were preferred to avoid the fishy smell lingering on the cutlery. Modern washing-up technology has done away with this necessity.

Crockery

Having a place plate in the centre of the cover ready to take the plate containing the first course is a good idea, particularly with soup or shellfish as it provides a resting-place for the spoon or discarded shells.

A small side plate should be placed on the left-hand of the cover. This is for bread, possibly table napkin, salad, or separate vegetables. If left empty is useful for anything you may need to be removed from the main plate. Should you or your guests find the odd fly in the soup, it can be discreetly transferred to the side plate, without causing too much fuss!

Fingerbowls, when necessary, can be placed on the left of the cover above the cutlery.

Butter dishes, sauceboats, and any similar items that are to be used by more than one guest should be added at the appropriate time and placed where they can be most easily reached or passed around by the guests.

Glasses

Glasses should be arranged in the order they are used. Therefore the water glass is normally placed nearest to the top of the right-hand side of the plate, above the tips of the knives, with first the white wine and then the red wine glass, grouped behind. If port, brandy or liqueurs are being offered these glasses can be added at the time of serving or can already be placed on the table, if room, at which time most of the glasses other than the water glasses would have been cleared away.

Table napkin

This can be placed either on the side plate, centre of the place setting or wherever most convenient.

Salt & pepper

Individual salt and pepper are placed either at convenient places along the centre of the table, or, if in ample supply to the left of each cover.

'*Eat, drink, and love;*
The rest's not worth
a fillip'

LORD BYRON

Sardanapalus

branch 6

catering

The catering equipment needed will largely depend on the venue's existing facilities. Therefore determine your requirements in an early stage of the planning so that you can be sure of obtaining – by purchase or hire – whatever is necessary.

KEEPING FOOD / DRINK COOL

If food is to be prepared in advance on the premises and some items of food and drink need to be kept cool this can be done, either by using cold-storage units hired or provided, or, alternatively reserve a small room or separate area specifically for this purpose. To assist in keeping the temperature low, use this space to store blocks of ice, although you will need to place them in large containers or bin bags to avoid a flood!

A closed bathroom with ice blocks placed in the empty bath is ideal, especially if you cover the bath with large trays, or a piece of cheap plywood on which to place the food.

HOT FOOD

The golden rule when serving hot food is that it should be hot! If the kitchen, oven, van or whatever is being used to provide hot food is located far from the dining area, you will need hot plates or heating units set up as near to the eating area as possible. Food for large numbers is especially prone to getting cold so the heating equipment must be sufficient and suitable for the numbers catered.

Having planned your menu well in advance, it is advisable to arrange a tasting with a discerning friend and invite creative criticism. This will also give you a chance to practise the co-ordination and preparation of the food and to decide how much is required. Draft an action timetable listing the items that can be brought and prepared in advance and those that need to be prepared at the last minute. Fresh food requires careful planning with maximum focus on keeping the dishes fresh once prepared. (This is where a plentiful supply of airtight containers and cold storage facilities will prove invaluable).

SUPPLIERS

Choose your food and drink suppliers carefully. They are normally experienced professionals and will be able to provide a wealth of advice and assistance, so it is worth going to the trouble of finding good ones.

It is important to:

- Check their website and compare with competitors
- Take time to build a good relationship
- Explain what you require and be explicit with details
- Be definite about your budget
- Ask advice and heed it – this is all part of the service
- Study their terms carefully
- Make certain everything is confirmed in writing

NO OF CANAPÉS PER HEAD?

If you are not sure how many canapés you may need, the following is a guide:
A reception lasting 1-2 hour: 6 – 8 canapés per person.
A reception lasting 2-3 hours: 8 – 10 canapés per person.
If a reception is planned to last longer, more substantial finger foods should be provided.

MENUS

Whilst a full guide to menus is beyond the scope of this book, if you are in doubt about putting together a suitable menu, and need inspiration, consult a good cookery book or ask a friendly chef. You could also contact a suitable caterer and enquire about menus.

Alternatively suggestions for breakfast, lunch, dinner, canapé and buffet menus, are readily available on the web with suggestions from most caterers.

Caterers can also offer impressive themed and specialist dishes and canapés, especially when imagination, originality, and trouble is taken with the presentation.

BREAKFAST

If guests arrive after dinner (from 10pm) then it is usual and courteous to offer something hot after midnight, especially if alcohol is being served.
A hot dish such as kedgeree with tea or coffee and toast is a splendid idea and easy to prepare.

As are, bacon butties or eggs – scrambled, poached or otherwise with or without the additional sausage, tomatoes and bacon or a vegetarian alternative.

Heated trays are a must and the old fashioned simple oriental type, heated with nightlights is good and perfectly adequate.

CAKE

Cake makers today take huge pride in their work and given a little encouragement can deliver the most amazing and incredible creations. For the Big Birthday extravaganza I organized at Cliveden House Hotel, Taplow, Berkshire for Dame Shirley Bassey's 70th I required something unique and brilliant. Eric Lanlard came up trumps and the result of his work is shown in the Collage of Cakes.

Most professional cake-makers require at least two to three weeks' notice to produce a special cake and wedding cakes take a great deal longer. When caught short I have found myself having to produce an instant Birthday cake with style. I have found the easiest and most effective solution is to buy simple, ready-made

An original and stylish idea. Christiane de Muller serves Canapés on an antique mirror at her Chateau in Giez Switzerland

oblong sponge cakes, from the supermarket. Then I join them together using honey or marzipan to form the required shape and cover the result with either ready made or real icing. I then finish with candles, adding the person's name using ready-to-use tubes of icing and a big bow tied around the entire cake.

CAKES

- George Shweiry, the Terrace, Hotel de Paris, Monte Carlo
- Caviar Cake? Capri
- Zandra Rhodes' 70th
- Confetti rains on Liz at the presentation of a surprise birthday cake created by Mona Al-Khatib
- A somewhat risqué slice of birthday cake. Speciality of The Don Restaurant in the City of London
- Eric Lanlard's creation for Dame Shirley Bassey's Birthday party at Cliveden
- Terence Cole blows out the candles on his 'Leo' Birthday cake
- Cousin Martin Brewer's 80th Birthday cake practically melted with all those candles
- The Cake I created for my daughter Tallulah in the shape of her band's camper van. Showing a home-made cake can be a success!
- Michelle Herbert's cake for Husband Larry's Birthday. As the founder of Pantone, this colourful creation was ingenious

DRINK

Serving good cocktails or drinks, quickly gets a party going and helps break the ice. However, due to driving restrictions and various other reasons, including health, there are an increasing number of folk who do not drink alcohol. They need consideration, so whatever drinks you decide to offer, remember to include plain water and soft drinks, avoiding carbonated drinks, now generally referred to as 'Osteoporosis or cancer in a can' and those with huge amounts of added sugar again thought to be 'diabetics in a can'!

Whether you decide to serve champagne, sparkling wine, red, white or rosé wine, beer, mixes, a delicious fruit or wine cup or cocktails, will depend on your personal taste and budget. If budget is limited then a fruit based wine punch, such as sangria is a good idea. Not only simple to prepare but guests can easily help themselves, from either a punch bowl or large jugs.

A good tip to remember is that the greater the number of guests, the simpler the choice of drink.

André, the Butler greeting guests with a 'Black Jamaican' Cocktail at Andrew & Theresa Robert's home at Tryall, Jamaica

Serving

Either serve guests as they arrive from trays of ready poured drinks – not too many glasses on a tray as this can be hazardous to carry.

Also chilled drinks should not be poured too far in advance otherwise they will be warm by the time guests arrive and, in the case of Champagne will have lost its sparkle.

Make certain your waiters, or friends if you have not hired staff, circulate with jugs or bottles to top up glasses.

Correct way to pour champagne

The trick with pre-pouring champagne is simply to fill the bottom of each champagne glass on the tray, no more than about 20 cm. Then when guests start to arrive, top up the glasses carefully, to within approximately 20 cm. from the rim of the glass. Filling the glasses to the top will cause the champagne to loose its bubbles and therefore taste rather flat.

Incidentally the correct way to fill a champagne glass is to tilt the glass and fill;

this prevents the bubbles from spilling over.

The Bar

Making life easier for you and all concerned is paramount when entertaining.

A dispense bar is a practical asset. Not only to keep all the necessary tools for serving and mixing drinks but also helps preserve order, especially if the drinks are a distance from the kitchen.

The Bar can also be the main focus of the gathering, where guests tend to mingle and meet.

Champagne fountain at Liz's
Christmas Party at
The MayFair Hotel, London

Setting up a dispense bar

FRIDGE with Ice compartment and or a separate icebox
Suitable table (trestle or collapsible picnic is ideal)
Tablecloth or sheet to hide the front of the bar/table and all that is
    stored beneath
Apron
Glasses
Jugs
Trays
Plastic bins or containers for storing bottles on ice and putting empties
Ice buckets or bottle coolers
Ice
Ice Maker
Corkscrew
Speed pourers if required for bottles
Bottle opener
Bottle sealers
Ice tongs
Can opener
Measuring cup
Drinking straws
Cocktail sticks for garnishes
Cocktail shaker – if serving mixes
Small sieve
Spoons
Knife
Scissors
Grater
Drip trays
A supply of clean water for rinsing glasses (if necessary)
Bins or basins for collecting drink discarded from glasses
Bin liners and cleaning utensils

KEEPING COOL

*Blocks or large bags of
ice can usually be ordered
and delivered from your
wine merchant, garage or
supermarket, catering
firm or even the
local fishmonger.
Blocks of ice are especially
helpful if you need to keep
quantities of drink cool.
The champagne supplier
will normally deliver the
champagne ready cooled
and will generally
include ice buckets.
For cooling wines etc., I
have successfully used
a baby's plastic bath, filled
with ice! Plastic or rubber
bins are also good.*

Rubber gloves or a pack of disposable hospital/builders rubber gloves

Teacloths and paper napkins

Rolls of paper towels

First-aid kit

Sufficient light

Torch

Nuts, olives, fresh mint, fruit or whatever ingredients or garnishes you or the barman require

A whistle or bell in case of emergencies, or should you need to make an announcement

Containers

If you don't have a suitable punch bowl then washing-up bowls are an alternative. The exteriors can always be disguised with fabric, large leaves, and cellophane or silver foil.

Jugs are necessary for water, soft drinks, iced tea etc.

Glasses

Your local wine merchant should hire or loan you sufficient wine glasses or tumblers, if you give him the drink order otherwise, a catering company will provide. You may find it easier and just as economical to buy cheap glasses either direct on line, or from a retail outlet, or reject shop (who often have large stocks of hotel 'seconds').

When considering size, it is preferable to avoid small glasses, as they will need constant refilling.

However glasses that are too large could be asking for trouble! So medium sized is generally the best choice.

PARTY DRINK & COCKTAIL RECIPES

A charming good friend, Ian Wisniewski, one of the world's foremost authorities on spirits and cocktails says in his informative, comprehensive book, *Party Cocktails*, published by Conran Octopus, "throughout the world, it is liquid refreshment that fuels our good times."

A comment with which I thoroughly agree!

In his book he details more than 170 recipes for every type of occasion – from all time classics such as Martinis to non-alcoholic cocktails and *even hangover cures!*

Ian has conducted many master classes in making and appreciating cocktails. I have been an enthusiastic attendee at most of these and received his degree, with honours, in cocktail making and tasting! My memory though, of the classes, remains somewhat blurred… in fact after the Martini class I believe I completely lost a day, having discovered that 'dirty Martinis' and 'straight up Margaritas' were my definite favourites.

The following recipes are taken from Ian's book:

Margarita

> Wedge of lemon
> Salt, for rim of glass
> Ice cubes for shaker
> 15ml (1 tbsp) blanco (white or silver) tequila
> 15ml (1 tbsp) cointreau (orange liqueur)
> 30ml (2 tbsp) lime juice

Wipe the lemon over the rim of a Martini glass to moisten it, and then dip the rim into the salt.

Into a shaker half-full with ice, pour the tequila, cointreau and limejuice, and shake well.

Strain the cocktail into the glass, being careful not to dislodge the salt.

Dry Martini

> Ice cubes for mixing
> 75 ml (5 tbsp) gin or vodka
> 20 ml (1 ½ tbsp) dry vermouth
> Strip of lemon zest or a green olive for garnish

Place a few ice cubes in a mixing glass, add the gin or vodka and the dry vermouth, and stir. Strain into a Martini glass and garnish with the lemon zest or olive.

Creating the perfect Martini, Dukes Hotel, St James Place, London

Sangria

(Makes about 5 litres / 9 pints)
Plenty of ice
2 litres (3 ½ pints) sparkling lemonade
3-4 750-ml-bottles red wine
100 ml (4 fl oz) vodka (some may use gin although I do not)
Caster sugar, to taste
2 oranges, bananas and apples, peeled and sliced
1 cinnamon stick

Place plenty of ice in a large bowl. Pour in the lemonade, red wine, gin and vodka. Sprinkle in the sugar to taste, stir, then add the fruit and cinnamon and stir again. Taste and sprinkle in more sugar if required, stirring well to dissolve it before tasting again. Serve in tall glasses

Hot glogg or punch

Ideally, this spiced and sweetened wine should be heated the day before (without the vodka) to allow the flavours to develop. When ready to serve, add the vodka and reheat gently.

(Serves 4-6)
1 bottle (750ml) red wine
2 cinnamon sticks
8 cloves
12 cardamom seeds
5 tsp caster sugar
150ml (5 ½ fl oz) vodka.
To serve: raisins and blanched almonds, with cinnamon sticks f desired

Drop a few raisins and blanched almonds into mugs or heatproof glasses. Set aside. Heat the wine and spices gently in a saucepan, stirring almost to the boil, then strain into the prepared mugs or glasses. Serve with cinnamon sticks, if desired.

WINES & CHAMPAGNE

Good wine does not need to be expensive – there are scme excellent inexpensive wines and champagnes. Talk to a local wine-merchant, taste his suggestions, and be guided by his expertise. Take time to research and contact wine suppliers, restaurants, or hotels and attend their wine tasting events. Believe me inferior quality wine can be a disaster especially for the heads of your guests the following day.

Champagne takes its name from the region of north eastern France where it is made; a sparkling wine, however bubbly, made anywhere outside this area is termed sparkling wine – NEVER CHAMPAGNE. When it comes to a special celebration you should try to stick to the real thing. If your budget, though, is seriously limited, then take the greatest care to choose one of the better sparkling wines, especially those with the description 'Methode Traditionale' or 'Methode Champenoise' on the label, as this is an indication that the wine has been made using the traditional champagne-making methods. Also serve ICE COLD!

STORING & SERVING

Serving wine correctly is as important as choosing wine ard, as my mentor on party drinks, Ian Wisniewski points out:

"The right serving temperature is crucial, as this has an important influence on the way a wine tastes. White wines should be chilled to promote their character. Red wines should be served at room temperature and allowed some time to 'Breath', either by decanting or by pouring a small amount into a glass to help the rest of the bottle 'aerate'. This helps the wine to reveal its full credentials. The appropriate style of glass should also be used, as this has an important influence on the way that aromas and flavours are conveyed: in order to breathe more easily a good red wine needs a larger breathing area so it requires the more open surface afforded by the larger rim; white wine is generally served in a smaller glass."

CHAMPAGNE

The champagne quality can be affected by the way it is stored and poured. I am grateful to the Hon Daniel Brennan, at Laurent-Perrier UK for the following advice:

"The addition of bubbles increases the need for good storage conditions and extra care when serving. Even the shape of a glass can have an effect on the intrinsic aromas and flavours of the champagne. Champagne bottles should be stored horizontally or vertically at 12-18 degrees C (53-64 degrees F) out of direct light. It should be served at 4.5 – 7 degrees C (40-50 degrees F). When pouring champagne, pour a little into each glass first, then return and top each one up to between two-thirds and three-quarters full. Pour it only when your guests are ready to drink: pre-poured champagne will lose its sparkle – the essence of champagne."

SOFT DRINKS

In recent years it has become necessary for people to limit their intake of alcohol. So always have a sufficient supply of soft drinks and fresh water available. It is generally a good idea to over order, in fact this applies to the drink in genera as it can always be returned or stored however, having a celebration dry-up, by running out of drink, could be a disaster.

Use jugs as they can be refilled and generally make dispensing easier.

WATER

Still or sparkling? Best to offer either. Filtered tap water is perfectly acceptable and helps the environment as the trillions of empty plastic bottles used to bottle water only add to the catastrophic ever-increasing world recycling problems.

If your event lasts many hours, there comes a time when guests have eaten and drunk sufficiently and then they usually need large quantities of filtered tap water, and a good idea is to serve with slices of cucumber or lemon.

'If music be the food
of love, play on'

branch 7

entertainment

MUSIC

Music can be a vital ingredient to the success of a significant event as it helps set the mood and is most effective in creating the right atmosphere. From a complete orchestra or light background music, to the rhythms of a DJ, there is tremendous scope and your selection needs careful planning.

Consider the timetable of the party or event and decide when the type of music or entertainment you have chosen, would be the most suitable. Gentle sounds such as a harp or the violin are obviously at their most effective during the early stages or quieter moments and will certainly be appreciated by guests who arrive promptly. As numbers increase and the chat gets louder, this music can be totally overpowered, so musicians need to know when to finish or if necessary be replaced with something louder.

Background music or sound
Background music should be exactly as described. In the background and merely

Singer Songwriter
Tallulah Rendall performing at
the Saatchi Gallery London

SOUND LEVELS

Music should be loud enough to create the required atmosphere, but not so loud as to assault everyone's eardrums. Guests enjoying conversations don't want to have to strain to hear above the blast of a sound-system. Neighbours should also be taken into consideration, and forewarned and whenever possible included.

'Spirit of Russia' Celebration, Russian musicians at the House of Lords entertaining Niki Cole and the Ambassador of the Russian Federation

loud enough to break the silence, but not so that it interferes with conversation. It is ideal to help avoid awkward silences at the beginning of an event, when first guests begin to arrive. Other appropriate times could be before, during or after the meal or during band or entertainment breaks.

Depending on the type and size of venue, live performers such as harpists, violinists, pianists, string quartet, wandering minstrels of even a 'one-man-band', can be excellent in setting the tone and enhancing the ambience. Consider also choosing sounds linked to your particular theme, for example, background noises of the jungle, birds, bells, or the waves of the sea.

DJ & live band

Choosing between having live music or a DJ (Disc-Jockey) or both will be dictated by budget and your personal preference. Personal recommendation is best, however there is a huge selection on line so make certain, whomever you select, they are reliable, and will provide your music of choice, at a fee to suit your budget.

In addition, obtain a number of reliable references and, if possible, hear or watch them perform at another event. Most will also provide you with a selection of their music so you can assess them before making any decision.

Whatever you decide, it is extremely unwise to proceed without researching thoroughly.

Where you position the DJ or musicians will depend on your venue. If space is limited make certain the equipment is set up in an area, which is safe and easy to access, and exit.

CABARET

Keep whatever cabaret is planned to within an agreed time frame. Guests in a party mood have a limited attention span so the golden rule is – keep it short!

However excellent the cabaret may be, there will come a point when guests wish to continue chatting and partying. Don't risk allowing them to become irritated or bored.

This applies also to the performer who obviously won't appreciate the lack of attention.

Occasionally getting the guests to participate, with magic shows, limbo dancing etc., can warm up the atmosphere. A surprise cabaret is always fun but again keep it short and sharp.

A singer who performs whilst mingling with the audience can also be highly entertaining and particularly flattering for the person being serenaded.

Choosing a comedian can be dangerous. Nothing will destroy your atmosphere quicker than flat jokes!

OTHER PERFORMERS

- Performers whose speciality is welcoming guests is a good way of putting them into the right frame of mind
- Buskers – who can be located usually near underground entrances or in some notable locations like Covent Garden, London. Some of these artistic performers occasionally end up as tomorrow's stars

SPOTLIGHTS

Special performers and cabaret artists benefit from spotlighting. Well-positioned lighting can make all the difference and enhance a performance. If this is required a good lighting technician can advise and supply.

- Magicians
- Balloon sculptors
- Face-painters
- Fortune tellers
- Living statues
- Stilt walkers
- Acrobats
- Clowns

The list is endless and any one of these can add an extra dimension and excitement to your gathering.

LIGHTING & SOUND SYSTEMS

Always check the power supply is sufficient for any extra load, when installing sound, light and control systems.

The amplifiers and sound boxes, need to be carefully positioned and directed where you wish the sound to be focused, leaving other areas, which could be more conducive to conversation, quieter.

When setting up your own sound system, you need to know exactly what you are doing, otherwise get expert advice and don't take any risks. Blowing up the sound system and ending up with no power would be horrendous – as could electrocuting yourself or any guest…

You may laugh but this was a lesson I learnt many years ago with one of the first Charity Balls I organised. It was bucketing down with rain and my electrician suddenly discovered that the power box had lost its cover and was almost filled with water – another few centimetres and the 300 guests and I would have been cinders!

DANCING

Always discourage guests from taking their glasses onto the dance area. Broken glass or a wet floor, is the most frequent cause of accidents. Should this occur, give

PERFORMERS FEES

Always agree a fee at the time of booking and before any contract is signed. Make certain the duration of the performance is agreed by both sides: the time they will begin and end and whether any short breaks are required. Also whether food and drink needs to be provided as well as any special insurance. If a performer has exceeded your expectations, it is perfectly in order to give an extra tip. There is no set amount just what you feel fair.

instructions to stop the music, clear the floor, and make certain the spillage or broken glass is cleared immediately.

It would seem no longer necessary to add to the above 'taking a lit cigarette on to the dance floor' however at a private function there is always some fool who may think it's cool! Fortunately, though, this habit has practically disappeared.

Make certain the DJ or musicians take on the responsibility of keeping an eye open for any mishaps and that you are instantly alerted. Also have a broom, mop, and fire extinguisher clearly visible.

Scottish reels or other group dances

Reels or group dancing are a traditional way in the UK of getting everyone to circulate and meet.

By including a few Scottish reels or some English country dancing can be enormous fun.

Scottish reels were in fact originally designed for this purpose: to give everyone a chance to meet or at least to dance with every guest. Many of the early English country-dances were also designed to encourage the young to dance with a variety of partners.

If you are not familiar with the various group dances then hire one or two professionals who will lead the guests through the steps.

Historical note re. English country dances arriving in America

English Country Dances in fact arrived in America with the first settlers in the early 1700s. They were the traditional social dance, and lasted, well into the 1800s. They are historically important, since they were the direct ancestors of the contra dance and the square dance, the two traditional dance forms of America. The contra dances were done in long lines with men on one side, and their partners across from them.

The English Country Dance was revived in America, with enthusiasm, in the 1940's due primarily to the influence of two school teachers from England, May Gadd and Genevieve Shimer, who brought the dance to their American students, as a means of teaching social graces and deportment, as well as rhythm and movement.

The dances were done in long sets, called 'longways sets', or in two, three,

PERFORMERS REQUIREMENTS

A room to change. If you do not have space, then a small tent could work, as could a screened-off area with mirror, chair, hook and hangers. WC facilities and refreshments. It sometimes is a bonus to give an entertainer a list of guests with notes & photos relating to a few guests so they can really take advantage of this knowledge and have some fun.

or four couple sets with slow and graceful dances, as well as exciting and energetic ones.

An English Country Dance is, also a great form of community dance, by which I mean, that they are fun to do, with no special training and can be learned by young and old alike. They are also good mixers, since partners have to change after every dance, resulting in a blend of sociability, mild exercise, and popular music. Perfect to relieve the isolation of today's fragmented high-tech society!

Dancing has recently had an enormous revival with the introduction of popular TV shows such as, 'Strictly Come Dancing' etc. Dance Studios such as those started by my lovely friend Debbie Moore, the Pineapple Dance Studios, are over-filled with those eager to learn everything from traditional Ballroom dancing to Salsa, other Latin American dances, Tango, Street Commercial Hip-hop, or even Pole dancing!

For some inexplicable reason the rumba continues to thrive – even at the more conventional dances. To join in you need to be feeling very stupid – or very intoxicated!

Dance Card

The quaintly old-fashioned dance card is still occasionally used at Hunt Balls and Grand Balls, especially in Scotland. It is a quaint but fun way of getting people to move around and meet each other during the evening.

Ensuring that everyone receives and uses the dance cards takes some organizing. The general rule is to give everyone his or her dance card on arrival with a small pencil attached. Printed on the card should be the number of the reel or dance followed by its name.

e.g.

1. The Dashing White Sergeant . . . . Clive Collins
2. The Eightsome Reel. . . . . Alick Hay
etc, etc.

The guests' then must choose different partners for all the named and numbered dances. Once a proposed dance partner has agreed, his or her name should be written alongside the number and name of the dance or reel.

The Dance Card

Guests have to make certain they nab their partners as quickly as possible in order to get their cards filled. It is then the duty of both parties to find their relevant partners before each dance.

It is an almost unforgivable faux pas, not to show for your requested dance. You may never live it down or be forgiven!

PARTY GAMES

Never underestimate the popularity of party games. They are also a good way of encouraging guests to communicate and bond. Charades is a typical example: the suggestion to play is often greeted with a few groans but once the game gets going, those guests, who may have heaved huge sighs, often end up by having the most fun and being extremely competitive.

One such occasion I will never forget whilst staying with friends in their glorious castle on the borders of Scotland. Following a seated black tie dinner for about 30 guests charades was announced. One particular guest, known for her somewhat formidable character and prim attitude, totally floored the entire gathering with her astonishingly, frank, and memorable interpretation of 'Fanny by Gaslight'! I don't think I need to add the details.

Charades
You will need paper, pencils/pens and a bowl, hat or other container.

Divide guests into two teams. Easiest way to do this is to choose two leaders who take turns to choose their teams from amongst the guests.

Decide on which subjects will be the topics, such as books, films, TV shows, and theatre.

One team goes into another room so both teams have privacy.

Each member of the team then has to think of an original title with the chosen categories, which is then written on a piece of paper, folded and put in the hat or container. It is a good idea to have a time limit for this of say, ten minutes, after which everyone returns to the main room.

A member of one of the teams starts. He/she is given or takes at random one of the folded slips of paper from the opposite team. Having discretely looked at what is written they then have to decide how to mime the word or words to their own team, so they are able to guess the answer, as quickly as possible. A set time is allowed for this.

To make it easier for the team to interpret the player's silent gesturing, the player will usually mime one word at a time or even syllable by syllable.

To make this easier still, there are some standard gestures as per the following:

- Book – opening both hands palms upwards as if opening a book.
- Film – using the hands to mime the action of an imaginary clapperboard.
- Play – using the hands to mime the drawing back of stage curtains.
- TV programme – by drawing a square in the air with the fingers.
- Number of words in the title – holding up the relevant number of fingers.
- First word – holding up one finger.
- Second word – holding up two fingers etc etc.
- Sounds like – by pulling the ear then miming the word that rhymes.
- Small word such as 'a', 'and', 'the', etc. by closing the thumb and forefinger.
- Whole title – by using both hands to draw a circle in the air.

If necessary long words can be broken up into syllables; if one word is particularly difficult to mime the player can move on to the next, hoping the team will not need it in order to guess the full title. Whatever happens the player must continue to be silent. They can indicate when someone gets a word right or wrong by nodding or shaking the head.

So, for example, if you were miming 'A Town Like Alice' you would open both hands to indicate a book and then mime the clapperboard to indicate that it had also been made into a film. You would then show four fingers indicating a title of four words and then one finger to show that you were going to describe the first word, which would be done by closing the finger and thumb together, indicating a tiny word. When your team guesses the first word you continue to the second, which could be mimed by pulling your ear (sounds like) and giving a frown, from which you might hope they'd guess 'town'. You'd continue in this way until your team shouts out the correct title.

Someone with a stopwatch would make a record of the time and you'd receive one point for a win. The game continues until each team had mimed all of their titles. The team with the highest score wins.

Sardines

This game needs a large house and perhaps a garden. It can be great fun and somewhat intimate – as I discovered when I once chose the largest bed in the house in which to flatten myself and hide. I was in southern Ireland at the time with a boyfriend called 'Bill'. Sadly our relationship never recovered from that particular bout of Sardines!

One guest is given five minutes to hide. The hiding place must be large enough to accommodate most of the others playing, either in the same space or near by. The remaining guests follow one by one seeking out the hiding place. If they find the person hiding they join him/her and remain silent until all but one of the players have found the hiding place. The last person to arrive is the loser – the winners are the rest who, by the end of the game, are naturally very close friends!

Murder in the Dark

There are several different versions of this game and the following version was invented by my friend Anton Kristensen, to spice up his infamous house parties when he had a cottage on the Althorp Estate.

Take identical pieces of paper, one for each guest and write the word 'Murderer' on one of them. All the pieces are then folded and placed in a hat or bowl and shuffled before asking each player to take one of the pieces of paper, which they then discretely read without letting anyone else see the content. At this point, only the person who draws the word 'murderer' will naturally, know who the 'murderer' is, or rather will be.

All the lights are then turned off and chosen doors closed to contain the game in a limited space. The players then stumble around the room or rooms, bumping into each other until the murderer is finally ready to commit the deed. This may be done in whatever way has been stipulated before play commenced. Usually this is with a huge hug and kiss. The victim then screams and lies down. The 'Murderer' then quickly moves away from the victim to assume an air of innocence before the lights are switched on. The object of the game is for everyone then, including the victim, to guess who the 'murderer' is. In doing this each person is allowed to ask three questions. Some people are recognizable by certain features, such as height, length of hair, and so on, so the art of the game is the 'murderer's' ability to fool everyone; if he is tall he might have moved around the room with legs bent; if slim he might have added a pillow and so on. A very silly game, yes, but… great fun with a great deal of inappropriate behaviour and generally rather sexy or at least it was when playing with the wicked Anton!

The Hat Game

This is a little like musical chairs and was taught to me by David & Elizabeth Coaten and their family many years ago at a Boxing Day Party. Each guest needs to have a hat, the more bizarre the hat the better. Guests stand front to back in a circle, and as the music plays they pass their hats backwards to the person behind. When the music stops, they must place whatever hat they happen to have in their hand on their head. Since the game will have started with one hat short, there will be one person hatless when the music stops. This person is 'out'! Each time this happens another hat is taken out of play so that there is always one hat short and the winner is the last person wearing a hat.

PYROTECHNICS & FIREWORKS

Fireworks definitely add brilliance to a celebration. Even a short blast of sophisticated fireworks is exhilarating, however, unless you really know what you are doing, or you have help from someone who does, it is best to bring in the professionals.
One thing to bear in mind is that with a fireworks display you do get what you pay for. So do not be tempted to go with a company that can offer an inexpensive 10 minute display… as you will be disappointed! In a nutshell, your budget dictates.

Search for a specialist company who will design a show to fit your budget, and fire it to music with perfectly synchronised fireworks. Make certain you are aware of what you are getting, be it Lancework (messages) or Fire Rope Set-Pieces displaying initials or names.

Make certain fireworks are stored safely, in a closed box, somewhere cool and dry, out of reach of children and animals, locked away until when they're needed.

Burlesque performing Tea Cup
entertains at one of
Tallulah Rendall's first
Album Launches

'It is –
what it is'

IVANA TRUMP

Celebrity Big Brother
2010

branch 8

staff and helpers

Efficient and adequate help is an essential factor, especially if you, as well as the guests, want to enjoy the occasion. If the people you may be hiring are new to you, then make certain you check their references thoroughly. An approved catering firm will have done this and made certain their staff are up to scratch, but you must do your research before the event as there is no point in protesting after, as you and most probably your guests will have a miserable time.

If your budget doesn't stretch to hired help then recruit a few close friends or their kids. Kids love to help, especially if you give them a little incentive! Friends also enjoy contributing, especially those who find parties daunting as it gives them a good reason to circulate in a natural way whilst helping you at the same time. If disaster strikes and you suddenly find yourself with no help then honesty is the best policy. Explain your predicament to early arrivals who will, with any luck, offer to muck in or may have someone they could get hold of at this time of crisis.

My 'just in case' tip is always to have a few fun aprons or even French maids outfits with which to deck out these helpful guests – giving a whole new slant to any party!

DOORMEN

It is advisable to have help with opening the main door when you are entertaining more than a few close friends. In this way you are able to look after and entertain your guests, make introductions and circulate.

If numbers attending are large then you will need a guest list (or two) on the door and a couple of helpers to check names of guests as they arrive.

I find people still lacking, when it comes to replying to an invitation and the occasional guest still turns up who has not had the good manners to reply. Also unbelievable as it may seem, guests who originally refused for whatever reason, then find they are able to attend but somehow omit to tell you!

I therefore have an extra guest list of guests in the following two categories:

Those who have not replied.
Those who have refused.

So if there is an unexpected arrival the guest is asked to wait until the extra list has been checked.

Irritating for them but hopefully a lesson learned!
Then are they admitted and the door control lets me know….

Waiters in Mona Al-Khatib's garden at Wentworth

CAR JOCKEYS

Car jockeys are also very useful, especially when the cars have to be parked some way from the venue. They will take the car from the driver on arrival, give him or her a ticket and take care of the parking efficiently and safely. When ready to leave the car jockey will on presentation of the ticket fetch and return your car. A tip is normally in order.

GREETERS

On occasions when there are a number of hosts, it is usual for them to line up at the entrance in order to greet guests as they arrive. If for whatever reason, the host/s is or are not familiar with all the guests then either a Master of Ceremonies (MC), or an official greeter can receive each guest on arrival, take the person's name and announce him or her to the host/s.

MASTER OF CEREMONIES & TOASTMASTERS

An experienced and competent MC is a bonus to a special event – an asset to the host not only in aiding the co-ordination and timing of the occasion but also in the following ways:

- Co-ordinating the timing
- Directing and announcing guests
- Occasionally saying Grace
- Proposing an appropriate toast (as directed)
- Announcing and introducing special guests, speakers and performers
- Making appropriate announcements such as:
    The Loyal Toast to the reigning monarch
    Request to remove a badly parked car
    Time to go home

BUTLERS

The main duty of a butler is to answer the door, announce the arrival of guests, and serve drinks. Nowadays the butler's duties are less clearly defined and extend to preparing the glasses, the drinks, the ice and even the canapés and making certain all is clean & tidy in the kitchen after the event (including the glasses). Butlers normally wear black tie or a dark suit and white gloves are sensible and a good idea for the obvious reason it adds to the reassuring impression of cleanliness.

COOK OR CHEF

With the current vogue of celebrity chefs teaching how simple it is to create tempting culinary wonders it is hard to believe there are still those, like myself, who are useless in the kitchen! To my shame the first time I attempted to cook when I was married, I set fire to the kitchen! Fire engines arrived alerted by a neighbour who had seen smoke billowing from the rear windows. At the time I was wallowing in my bath, having totally forgotten the rather nasty block of frozen spinach, I was attempting to cook in a saucepan. I haven't really improved which is why at home I eat raw!

If you decide to use the full services of a professional catering company all will be taken care of and you will merely need to give your preference as to menus etc. However if you decide to take on the catering yourself, or employ the services of a cook/chef and other help to assist you in the kitchen you will need to know the extent of their capabilities. References are essential and hopefully they come highly recommended, from a specialist agency. However, good staff, are a rare commodity nowadays, and therefore it may be worth using the services of companies who do an upmarket type of meals on wheels service. Alternatively a catering school may be able to assist with one of their students.

Whatever you decide, have a trial run and tasting – after all, you do not want to find out at the last moment that all they can create in the kitchen is, havoc!

WAITING STAFF

Waiters and waitresses either are booked through the caterers, specialist agencies or the recommendation of friends. Even a local restaurant may help out with prior warning. If you are hiring direct, the charges are generally by the hour, plus an amount for travel if they need to work late.

They do not automatically come with uniforms so it is advisable to enquire what they usually wear and what you would prefer them to wear. If you require a particular uniform, then you may have to supply or cover the cost of hiring it.
It is also a good idea to check the applicant's nails. Dirty nails are unhygienic and give a very bad impression to the guests.

CLOAKROOM & LAVATORY ATTENDANTS

Anything over twenty coats and jackets can cause havoc when guests leave. There is also the risk that a coat may leave on the wrong back, a frequent occurrence at a good party. It looks the same, feels the same but the following morning the horrifying realization that it is not yours! Even worse when you finally arrive home to discover someone else's house keys or even car keys in the pocket.

So hiring a professional cloakroom attendant or your kids or a friend to help keep order, with taking the coats is essential.

Easiest way is to set aside a hanging rail, with numbered hangers at the ready, using one half of a raffle ticket and the other half given to the coat owner.

CLEANERS

Unless you have hired professional caterers, who automatically clean up after the event, arrange for help with the clearing up, as having to do this chore, after a particularly wonderful, wild celebration, can really throw a damper on the whole joy of hosting.

There are companies who specialise in this and also individual cleaners so take advantage of their service.

I have for the past ten years or so co-hosted a professionally catered picnic luncheon for a hundred or so guests at Royal Ascot. Oh the joy of walking away at the end of the party knowing all will be immaculate, without even a trace of a champagne cork, when I return to my car at the end of the day's racing.

So make certain you have sufficient hands to help with this chore, as soon as possible, after the last guest departs.

Preparing for our Royal Ascot picnic in the No 1 Car Park

'*Welcome the coming, speed the parting guest*'

ALEXANDER POPE

Odyssey
Book 1

branch 9

the morning after the night before!

Don't underestimate the amount of debris that is always left after a good party. The huge trail never ceases to amaze me – though it does mean a great time was had by all.

If, for whatever reason, you have decided not to have professional help with the clearing up then my suggestion is – have a clearing up brunch. There are bound to be edible and liquid left-overs for all, and lets face it, you might as well enjoy yourself whilst doing, what would otherwise be, dreary after party chores. It helps if you have kept everything clean and orderly during the initial setting-up process and as much as possible during the event.

A vacuum cleaner, dustpan, and brush, brooms, mop, dusters and of course bin bags/liners are the essentials to have on hand. Bin bags are perfect for not just collecting the mess, but also for gathering the dirty linen ready for washing, and storing the remains of the décor for another occasion.

RETURNABLES

Return all equipment etc as soon as possible. If an item is damaged whilst in your care, check with your insurance company to see whether this is covered and inform them and the supplier immediately. This is not only courteous but the correct procedure. When using a catering company there is normally a charge for breakages and whether or not this is imposed will depend on your relationship with the company.

PHOTOGRAPHS

Either hire a professional photographer and give exact instructions as to the type of photos you prefer or allocate a friend to take photographs. Normally photos would include:

- Everyone on arrival either in couples or singly
- A record of the venue, table settings, etc
- Photos of the host/s
- Photos of the entertainers/band/DJ
- Highlights of the event
- The invitation/menu/guest list etc

The above list creates good ingredients should you wish to create an album on line for all your guests to enjoy or hard copy as a memory of a significant occasion.

LOST PROPERTY

Inevitably items go missing and there is always someone who leaves something behind (even before now, their spouse!) So make certain during the clearing up process all items are listed and stored carefully, in the hope that the owner makes contact when they discover their loss.

If the item is valuable, it is best to inform the local police, as occasionally the item is not missed for some time and the owner may forget where it could have

RELAXING

After any strenuous event an excellent way to recover and unwind is to spoil yourself and treat yourself to a really good massage Relax and relive all the high points of your party, in your mind.
When I do this I usually make notes of anything that I could improve upon in the future.

been lost. For insurance purposes the owner would have to report to the police, who, it is hoped, will connect the lost item to the owner.

'Celebration is the core curriculum of humanity'

LIZ BREWER

branch 10

duties of the host

LOOKING AFTER THE GUESTS

A host's duty is to look after the guests and although this may appear obvious, it is extraordinary how often this duty is overlooked.

Guests should be greeted and made to feel comfortable. It is not good enough to merely greet them with:

"Good to see you – enjoy yourself", or
"Hello – have a drink, I'm sure you'll know loads of people here and I'll catch up with you later."

How often have you arrived at an event not knowing a soul and felt really awkward?

Guests should never be left stranded to fend for themselves. As a guest, if you don't have a huge amount of confidence, there is nothing worse than arriving in a room full of people you do not know. Even if you are capable of plucking up enough courage to introduce yourself, you may end up feeling even more awkward: the

British still regard the unsolicited approach as an invasion of their space and may be less than truly welcoming, or worse, condescending.

If an incident occurs, concerning conversation or actions of guests, the host should smooth ruffled feathers in a diplomatic way and use whatever means possible to minimise the mishap, even perhaps with a light-hearted joke to quickly diffuse the atmosphere.

At one time, when I was helping some Turkish friends of mine who were hosting HRH Prince Phillip at a Charity event, taking place at the British Embassy Residence in Istanbul. It was noticeable that the service was exceedingly slow. We had been waiting after the pudding with dirty plates on the table for a considerable time. Finally a guest on the top table, where I was seated, started to quietly stack the plates. There was a look of grave concern on several faces – and a remark made, that stacking plates was considered impolite.

His Royal Highness aware of the concern, immediately started to help stack the plates and pass them to an embarrassed waiter, remarking,

"Why not? We often do this back at my home!"

Demonstrating a charming and sensible example of diffusing an awkward moment.

Circulating & introducing guests

The ability to circulate guests is an important ingredient of being a successful host. If, moving people around and making introductions is not a natural gift, then the required skills needs to be mastered.

A good host will move from group to group, adding a new sparkle to the conversation and making introductions where necessary, aiding the atmosphere and putting people at ease.

If a guest is standing alone the host should either personally introduce him or her around. Alternatively, if the host is occupied, they should summon a friend to subtly do this kind deed.

At any gathering the mingling of guests need to be kept dynamic and positive.

Today, it is not unusual to have either a friend with the necessary panache, or a specific person or team, employed to act in this capacity; moving people around and making certain everyone is happy and being looked after.

Introductions

As a general rule, the host should introduce a younger person to an elder, a man to a woman, a junior rank to a senior rank and so on. For example, 'Mary, this is John' or more formally 'Mary Smith this is John Brown' or Mary Smith (older guest) may I present (or introduce) Jane Brown (younger guest).

When making an introduction to a titled guest, it is usually safest to use the formal social address, leaving the titled person to diffuse the introduction such as:

"Lord Snooks may I introduce Jane Brown?" "Jane – Lord Snooks"

Lord Snooks then has the opportunity of interjecting "Hello Jane – John Snooks" or even a nod of the head "John Snooks, delighted to meet you Jane" to which Jane could respond with either "how do you do?" or merely "delighted to meet you."

Note that the phrase "how do you do?" under no circumstances requires you to start telling them, how you do. This is merely a courtesy acknowledgement and simply another oddity of the British language. The enquirer is not in the least interested in how your big toe may be hurting or the state of your piles! (Although, so saying, that is for some curious reason, very much a British male topic!)

Today introductions are done far more informally and are the means in which to convey a name, but at the same time put the person at ease. However it is important to speak clearly to ensure that both parties hear the other's name – it is embarrassing to ask someone to repeat their name after having only just been introduced.

Further on I have given basic information, concerning forms of address.

The art of making conversation

This could of course, fill a few chapters however basically, as the host, you would normally have the advantage of knowing who the majority of your guests are and therefore in a position to blend them together, using an appropriate conversation starter, such as:

"Ian, I believe you are a great believer in naturism and the glorifying of the naked body, well, Liz here believes modesty is a virtue and known to be revered by the great philosophers, such as Aristotle and Rousseau, and mainstream religions, so perhaps you could alter her point of view?"

Or something like:

"Terence loves fine furniture, especially tables, well – Niki loves dancing on them, so you two may have a great deal in common"

Having said your bit to break the ice, swiftly move on. If you can say something witty or amusing it will give them something to laugh and continue to chat about.

The art of good conversation is in knowing how to listen rather than talk. So learn to make others talk and take a genuine interest in what they have to say. The more you listen, the more you will find questions springing up to prevent the conversation drying up. If occasionally you find yourself out of your depth, never be afraid to ask questions: often the person speaking will be flattered by your interest, although don't play too helpless (especially if a woman) as this could be irritating.

DEALING WITH DIFFICULT SITUATIONS

Drunken guests

Irritating in the extreme, but a drunken guest needs to be dealt with gently and firmly and removed with as much discretion as possible. Either, leading them into a spare room or outside, and call a cab or a friend to take them home, immediately.

Do this quickly and with a degree of authority to avoid any unpleasantness.

An awkward guest

Be at your most diplomatic. If you think someone is about to make trouble and ruin a good atmosphere then guide the person firmly away to another group of people in the hope that the incident will be forgotten.

Another ploy is to apologise on behalf of the guest and immediately change the subject, including yourself in the conversation. If the awkward guest persists in being annoying and is determined to cause trouble then ask them to leave.

Gatecrashers

Gatecrashing is quite an art and it never ceases to amaze me how people have the audacity to turn up uninvited. However there are many people who have perfected the tricks of gaining access to private and public events and go to unbelievable lengths to gatecrash a good party especially if it is a 'hot ticket'.

Most of them are undesirables and more often than not, a bunch of freeloaders who contribute nothing to the occasion. If they were worth inviting they wouldn't need to resort to gatecrashing.

Occasionally this happens innocently, such as when an invited guest arrives with an unexpected friend. However if someone arrives, whom you neither recognize nor know the best policy is to take them to one side and ask them if they have an invitation. From their response you ought to be able to assess whether this is a genuine mistake. If it is, do not be embarrassed, the situation can generally be rectified, and no harm will have been done. However if the person has gatecrashed you have every right to politely ask them to leave, explaining that this is a private occasion. If they resist, which does happen – as in my experience gatecrashers are incredibly thick skinned – get help from a suitable strong-armed guest or in extreme cases call the police.

HOSTESS GIFTS & GOODY BAGS

Hostess gifts

Hostess gifts originally were made popular in the US and continental Europe. They are especially welcoming for guests who have travelled far and are staying in a house party or nearby accommodation.

For a significant celebration, such as a wedding, which may extend over two or three days, the gift could be left with the itinerary of planned activities as well as a welcome greeting from the host or hostess and a few items useful for their extended stay.

This type of consideration always makes a good impression.

Goody bags

Filling them yourself, is naturally preferable, however time consuming. However, there are companies on line, who specialise in providing luxury and celebrity goody bags, who can be guided by the theme or provide contents appropriate for the occasion.

Kids

Filled party bags for kids are available on line – are very reasonable and you'll find there is a good selection including themed ones specifically for boys and or girls.

Farewell to guests

If everyone is having a good time, it is not easy to terminate the festivities, even if the departure time is clearly indicated on the invitation – so, here are a few helpful tips to encourage guests to leave:

- So long as you are not overstepping the mark with the time limit for your helpers or staff, make an announcement to the guests saying that as everyone is having such a good time you have decided to extend the party by another half-an-hour (or whatever convenient). They will then get the hint.
- Announce how much you have enjoyed entertaining them and that you hope to see them again soon but it is sadly time to say farewell. This needs to be done in a light way with some humour.
- Ask the waiting staff or your helpers to gently guide guests to get their coats. The majority will soon get the message.
- Stop the drink being served and have the glasses politely collected while you move around, explaining to individual groups how delighted you were to share your party/celebration or whatever, with them and that you'd like to say a personal 'goodbye' to each of them.
- However you terminate things, make certain it is done in such a way, not to put a damper on the atmosphere.

DUTIES OF THE GUEST

Replying to the invitation

Whatever form the invitation takes it is the guest's DUTY TO REPLY.

It is thoughtless to leave your reply to the last minute and unforgivable not to respond at all! This is especially important if you cannot attend. The host needs to know whether they can invite a replacement and also the number for catering purposes. CULPRITS are nearly always those who don't entertain and therefore are unaware of all the complications, presented due to people being inconsiderate in this way.

E.g. arranging a dinner for 200 guests generally requires sending a proportion of invitations to doubles and the remainder to singles. When people fail to RSVP or reply it is impossible to know where you stand as far as attendees are concerned.

Before now I have sent out a large number of invitations and found that a week before the big day only 50% have replied. I have then had to send messages and make calls to sometimes a hundred or so potential guests, to find out, diplomatically, if perhaps the invitations did not arrive and whether they can or cannot attend. I now know every excuse possible for not having replied! Not replying makes the organizers life exasperatingly difficult.

Bringing a guest

Check First!

If you are invited as a single and wish to bring a friend you should inform your host and ask if this is possible. It is inconsiderate and bad manners to turn up with an unexpected guest and can cause embarrassment and inconvenience, especially if the event is seated or the numbers restricted.

Also do not assume that your guest is not known to the host, it may well be that he/she is their least favourite person!

Invited as a couple

Similarly if you have been invited as a couple and one of you cannot attend – INFORM YOUR HOST. They need to know, especially if their numbers are an important consideration.

Arriving with a present

Give some forethought to giving a present to your host and remember it is not always the cost of the gift that matters but the trouble and personal care it shows you may have taken. Even those people you feel may have virtually everything will be touched by a small personal gift with an original touch. Stylish presentation is also important. The way your gift is wrapped and tied, can add a glamorous touch.

Make certain your card is securely attached as so often the gift card falls off, leaving the host in the dark as to who gave the gift.

Giving wine if you are a guest at a dinner or cocktail party is a friendly idea but only if it is good quality. Thinking you can get away with a bottle of plonk will not be appreciated!

Also if you do bring a bottle of wine or champagne, do not expect your wine to be served. A good host will normally have selected and prepared appropriate wines for the occasion.

Timing

Unless instructed otherwise, it is normal to arrive approximately ten to thirty minutes after the time stated on the invitation, although this also depends on the type of occasion.

It is incorrect and inconsiderate to arrive before the time indicated. On the other hand to arrive noticeably late is bad manners, especially if the occasion is seated – so you had better have an excellent excuse.

If arriving late or early is unavoidable, you need, if possible to warn your host, and your arrival needs to be done discretely and with the minimum amount of disruption.

Knowing when to leave

Heed the golden rule:

Don't overstay your welcome!

Observe the departure time indicated either verbally or written on the invitation. Indicating the departure time is so that the host or organizer can alert the waiters or general staff and helpers, the amount of time they will be required. So your consideration is needed and if it is getting late, mention that you ought to be leaving – it is then the hosts prerogative to persuade you to stay.

When leaving it is unnecessary to bid everyone goodbye, a general farewell is sufficient, however, a personal thank you before you depart to your host or hosts should be done.

Thanking the host

Showing your appreciation to your host after receiving hospitality should be a priority. Even having thanked your host verbally, does not absolve you from sending flowers, or a written thank-you, be it hand-written, email, text or similar modern day communication.

Put yourself in the place of the hosts – the following day, or days after, wondering whether your guests enjoyed your occasion. The silence can be cruel and inconsiderate. So don't waste time: do it as soon as possible and if you did enjoy the occasion then say so and be as convincing and charming as possible. The longer you leave it, the harder it gets, and it will also lose meaning.

If you did not enjoy the occasion and consider thanking hypocritical – then fine, omit the thank you, although, you may not be re-invited. (Possibly, your preference!)

If you were a guest accompanying an invitee, write personally. Do not leave it to the invitee. One obvious reason for this, apart for being polite, is, it will give the host the means to contact you should they wish you to invite you again.

'formal, semi-formal cocktail, dark suit, lounge suit, informal, active attire, smart casual, business...'

appendix i

dress codes

Choosing appropriate clothes for a significant event can be a minefield as dress codes are often misleading or interpreted in various ways, although in different areas of society the rules may also differ.

Dress codes, for men, are fairly simple, and generally dictate the form of dress for women.

So unless a man wishes to demonstrate his own individual flair, he needs to merely follow the dress code instructions.

All formal dress for men require most of the following, depending on individual taste and the degree of formality:

Dinner suit, tuxedo or dinner jacket, trousers, shirt, tie, gloves, evening scarf, clean handkerchief, socks, cufflinks, studs, cummerbund, footwear, decorations & orders or other accessories.

As for women this needs more guidance.

FORMAL DRESS FOR MEN

The following, is a suggested guide for a formal occasion when the indication is, BLACK TIE.

Dinner suit/dinner jacket
Single-breasted dinner suit

A dark, generally black dinner Jacket with ribbed silk facings

White or preferably ivory evening jacket (for warm climates and in the US & Canada only from Memorial Day in the Spring to Labor Day), has self-faced rather than silk faced lapels (unlike the dark dinner jacket) and is worn with black trousers.

Velvet smoking jacket.

Historical fact
See blue columns.

Trousers
Suitable Black trousers, with or without black ribbon side trim with flat front or the old fashioned pleated version.

Tartan trousers – worn generally in Scotland, and by those who have a claim upon a tartan.

Breaches again worn in Scotland in preference to the kilt (See – Highland Dress).

Shirt
Dress Shirt

Cotton, liner or silk

The more traditional white, formal dress shirt, has a standard turn down collar, and fastens with matching studs and cufflinks.

The more conventional front is usually Marcella and can be pleated or plain.

More informal is the buttoned shirt with or without a fly front but if the buttons are visible then they should preferably be mother of pearl.

Tie

Black, silk, or alternative Bow Tie (preferably NOT pre-tied).

Or Hollywood black tie, (a classic knotted tie in black)

'Black tie – no tie' was introduced by David Cameron, at one of his early summer fund-raising Balls, before he was elected Prime Minister. The men literally wore no ties and most of those who did removed or undid them to hang loose.

Socks

Traditionally black fine wool or silk or according to personal choice.

Gloves/evening scarf

As you wish!

Military, or Civil, decorations and orders

The invitation's dress code normally dictates whether these are to be worn.

Traditionally, they are worn to a full dress formal event, connected either to the state, or sovereign.

They are normally positioned on the left lapel or left breast of the jacket.

Medallions, pins or sashes are worn according to the relevant country's regulations or individual requirements.

Hats

In recent years celebrity culture has adopted hats as part of their look or personal style, especially amongst the younger and trendier set.

It is however, still good manners to either remove your hat in the presence of women, or at least doff the hat as a sign of respect.

Hats are not worn indoors, during a black tie event – however cool the look may be!

Cufflinks/studs

Cufflinks & Studs: Preferably in gold, black, or possibly silver settings, can feature onyx or mother-of-pearl and have various geometrical shapes e.g. circles, octagons, squares, or rectangles. Studs are recommended for a dress shirt.

formal dinner wear at that time), in preference to a new style of smoking jacket without tails, which the Prince had requested be designed by Henry Poole.

On returning to America, James Potter's new dinner suit proved such a winner at The Tuxedo Park Club; they made this their new mode of dress for dinners. It transpired that one of their members, wore this tail less dinner jacket at a Ball outside of the Tuxedo Park Club, and another diner questioned, why this fellow's jacket had no coat-tails, the explanation given was:

"He is from Tuxedo Park". Thus the name 'Tuxedo' stuck and now appears to represent any type of formal or semi-formal dress including white tie and morning dress!

George Piskov, Chairman
of Uniastrum Bank and founder
of Unistream Money Transfers,
with Lord Lamont in
Black Tie at a
House of Lords dinner

Handkerchief
Clean white – Silk or cotton.

Waistcoat/vest
Waistcoat (UK) Vest (US): if worn this can be an expression of your own personality therefore design is a matter of personal taste.

In the US and warmer climates, as it has become increasingly common for men to remove their jackets, the waistcoat or vest, are now frequently designed with a full back.

Cummerbund
On the wane, though still occasionally worn (hoping to hide large stomachs perhaps?)

However avoid at all cost matching the coloured cummerbund and tie variety!

Footwear
Black shoes, lace-up (considered very informal), or pumps

Velvet monogrammed slippers. (Generally worn on home ground!)

The most formal for evening are patent leather court shoes.

BLACK TIE FOR WOMEN

Normally the 'Dress: Black tie' for women code, will depend on the type of occasion.

For a seated dinner without dancing a long or short slim gown is in order.

However if dancing is indicated, then a simple ball gown either long or short is correct – unless long gown is indicated.

Evening trousers for women began to make an appearance in the 20's and then again towards the end of the last century, and now frequently appear at black tie events, although they do not really beat the elegance, style and romance of an evening skirt or gown.

SCOTTISH HIGHLAND & LOWLAND DRESS

Worn at white tie and black tie occasions, hunt balls, Scottish reels and céilidhs, but ONLY when the wearer has claim to a clan. Otherwise black tie is acceptable at formal balls in both the highlands and lowlands.

Highland dress comprises the following:

- Black barathea jacket with silver buttons
- Regulation doublet or black mess jacket
- Matching waistcoat/vest
- Kilt in relevant tartan
- White shirt with studs and turn down collar
- White lace jabot or hand tied black bow tie
- Evening dress/black Gillie brogues
- Kilt hose – tartan or diced.
- Silk flashes or garter ties
- Dress sporran with silver chain
- Black silver-mounted Sgian dubh

Lowland dress is similar to the normal black tie but generally includes tartan trews, or black silk breaches rather than black tie trousers, and could include a Prince Charlie jacket instead of the dinner jacket.

Women

wear long evening gowns preferably with swirling skirts, in which to reel. If er titled, a tartan sash worn diagonally across the shoulder to the waist is worn according to their clan. The way the sash is tied will depend on her married status. Normally the wife wears the husband's tartan.

Appropriate evening shoes are vital and need to be comfortable for dancing the numerous, boisterous reels.

Alick Hay of Duns wearing
Sheriffmuir Jacket with
Hay tartan evening trousers
and Angus Hay in
Hay Tartan Dinner Jacket
(or smoking jacket) at
The Berwickshire Hunt Ball,
Duns Castle

George & Tanya Piskov hosting
their luncheon at Royal Ascot

COCKTAIL DRESS – MEN & WOMEN

Men

For a man this indicates either a dark suit or lounge suit, or even smart blazer and trousers, unless he is continuing to a more formal event. If that were the case, then the dress code for that event would take precedence.

Women

If the invitation states something like – 'Cocktails 7pm' then dress smart with style and wear what you consider would suit the occasion. If, on the other hand, the dress code is, 'Cocktail dress' then this tends to indicate something smarter and wearing a cocktail dress or similar would be advisable.

Cocktail parties, unlike drinks parties, which indicate a far more informal occasion, show an effort is being taken and therefore it is gracious to your host to make an effort in your presentation and dress. After all, early evening cocktails often progress to dinner or whatever so best to be ready for any eventuality.

Smart/casual is very misleading; however if this is stated on the invitation, go for being stylish, as looking good is really what is meant by this description.

Informal

Informal, as a dress code, is tiresome and the host deserves all the irritating messages enquiring what this actually means. Best to avoid this on invitations and stick to being explicit as to what you would like your guests to wear, and what you feel most appropriate for the occasion.

WHITE TIE

Men

If white tie is indicated on an invitation, this means a grand occasion and the dress code is far more rigid.

A black tailcoat, (not to be confused with a morning coat), starched white shirt, with detachable stiff winged or stand-up collar, white bow tie, white waistcoat, both preferably with mother-of-pearl studs, black evening trousers and black evening

Liz at a White Tie Ball
in Scotland

shoes or opera pumps with a grosgrain bow.

Decorations are always permitted when white tie is worn.

In the event that white tie is not part of your wardrobe, or available, then Black tie is permissible – however the wearer will stand out, so it is preferable to either hire or borrow.

Women

White tie indicates long evening gown or long evening skirt. Trousers, however well designed are not appropriate.

Long evening gloves can be worn with sleeveless gowns, although this is no longer a necessity.

Tiaras can be worn although are no longer obligatory, unless indicated, and the tradition that married women should only wear them, has long been forgotten.

Alick Hay of Duns in his dining room at Duns Castle, prior to The Berwickshire Hunt Ball

MORNING DRESS

Men

The normal attire in Britain for weddings, Royal Ascot, state and civic grand occasions, indicates a frock coat or morning coat. For those completely baffled, this is the coat which somewhat resembles the look of a penguin! NOT to be confused with a tailcoat as worn with white tie which is cut differently.

A grey coat is worn with matching grey trousers.

Traditionally worn with a plain shirt, waistcoat, white collar – preferably starched and striped, fancy or hound's-tooth trousers plus plain black shoes with laces.
It is correct to wear a top hat either in grey, or black silk and this can depend on the colour of the coat.

Women

The requirement is to be elegantly dressed in either a stylish suit or beautiful dress with fashionable hat, gloves, shoes, and handbag.

Wearing a suitable jacket or coat to compliment the outfit depends upon the weather.

HUNT BALLS

Men

Tailcoats, red or otherwise, are worn if the wearer is a member of the hunt; otherwise black tie or white tie, if stipulated, is appropriate.

Red tailcoat is worn with starched white shirt, white waistcoat, (both with studs), white bow tie and black patent shoes.

Don't make the mistake of borrowing or wearing a red tailcoat without knowing which hunt it signifies. Be aware that each hunt has its own special buttons and the collar lining and facing generally have a distinctive colour. It could be awkward if someone enquired about the buttons and you did not know which hunt they represented.

As with white tie, decorations can be worn.

Women

Preferably a long or three-quarter length full gown – after all this is a Ball rather than a dance, and a great deal of swirling and whirling is done during the dances. A tight slim gown will prove embarrassing and restrictive and such traditions as the Horn Blowing Competition' demand nothing too revealing with the décolleté.

Shoes should be comfortable and attractive – enabling you to enjoy the dancing.

BUSINESS DRESS

Business, in today's world is ever-increasingly revolving around a person's technical equipment and technical ability and offices are frequently situated on home ground.

In the financial world a dark suit and tie is still worn for meetings but generally not in the office.

In the more creative industries, open neck shirts, T-shirts or more casual wear have taken over, although, there is a definite underlying accent on individuality and style.

Where once, 'dress down Friday' was the end of week normal uniform, now on a daily basis, comfortable, stylish relaxed clothes are worn, unless a meeting or contact with a client is planned.

ATTENDING A SPORTS EVENT

e.g. Tennis, Cricket, Polo, Golf tournaments, etc

What to wear, depends on the type of invitation received.

If invited by the sponsor to attend a morning, afternoon, day or evening event, which includes hospitality, then in respect for your hosts you should dress accordingly and make an effort, at the same time take comfort and weather into consideration.

Shoes depend on the type of ground you will be walking over and as in the case of Polo, whether you will be 'treading in' the divots, which is all part of the tradition of the sport.

A sun hat is necessary at any outside occasion, especially if you find you are seated in the sun.

A HISTORICAL POINT

Originally it was the tradition at the end of every round of golf for men to shake hands and then remove their caps, as a mark of respect for their opponent. This continues today.

APPROPRIATE DRESS

- The Queen arriving at Royal Ascot
- Ivana Trump, Valerie Ilinich with the hosts George & Tanya Piskov at their Luncheon in the No 1 Car Park at Royal Ascot
- Lord Northbrook, Justin Cadbury, Tanya Piskov, Olga Palkina and Anders Wernsten at The Prince's Drawing School Clay Shoot
- Liz, fly fishing on the Test
- Niki Cole & Liz at Holland & Holland's Shooting Ground
- David Bond, Clive Leigh Collins, Liz with James Bond and his mother Ina at Royal Ascot
- HRH Prince William of Wales with fellow members of his Polo Team at Lord & Lady Lloyd Webber's country estate, Watership Down
- Ian & Victoria Watson enjoy Picnic Luncheon in the No 1 Car Park at Royal Ascot
- Holland & Holland's model with Christopher Biggins at a Clay shoot to benefit The Prince's Drawing School
- Lisa Tchenguiz and Steve Varsano at Liz's Luncheon party at Royal Ascot hosted by George & Tanya Piskov
- Leander Cadbury and his father Justin with Karen Malayan at Holland & Holland's Shooting Ground
- Lucinda Watson and team at the Ladies Tournament with the sponsor David Singleton
- Valentina Kristensen and her mother Isabell at the Piskov's luncheon at Royal Ascot
- A very stylish Gemma Sheppard relaxing elegantly between stands at The Prince's Drawing School Clay Shoot

Addressing English Royalty

King or Queen
Your Majesty...
  thereafter Ma'am

Prince or Princess
Your Royal Highness...
And thereafter
Sir or Ma'am

appendix ii

forms of address

The way you address someone, should depends on the degree of your friendship and relationship with that person.

As a rule the addressee should be formally styled on an envelope, regardless of how well you may know them.

How you address them on email or text again depends on how well you know them and this should apply to all forms of modern day written communications.

For example receiving a written communication from someone you have never met, addressing you in a familiar manner can be startling, and could be considered presumptuous! The sender may consider this a friendly gesture; however there is an old saying that 'familiarity breeds contempt' and this can often be the case.

Whitaker's Almanac, Debrett's or Wikipedia can be a great help in checking correct usage when addressing titles etc. So when in doubt, it is best to check.

The following is a short guide:

MEMBERS OF THE ROYAL FAMILY

When writing to, or replying to, members of the Royal Fam ly, you should correspond with the individuals' Private Secretary.

In making introductions, you present a person to a member of the British Royal Family.

The Queen or King

Addressing in person: Your Majesty, thereafter 'Ma'am' (pronounced Marm), or 'Sir'.

Making an introduction: 'Your Majesty, may I present….'

Addressing a communication: The Private Secretary to Her Majesty, The Queen or His Majesty, The King.

Starting the communication, to the Private Secretary either, Dear Sir or Dear Madam, having first checked to find which is relevant, or their name, if known.

ROYAL CONSORTS

Royal Princes and Princesses

Addressing in person: 'Your Royal Highness', thereafter 'Sir', or Ma'am.

Making an introduction: 'Your Royal Highness, may I present…

Addressing a written communication: The Private Secretary to His or Her Royal Highness (followed by the full title, e.g. The Princess Royal, The Duke of York, Prince Michael of Kent.

Again addressing the Private Secretary with Dear Sir or Madam or their actual name if known.

PEERS OF THE REALM

Dukes and Duchesses

Addressing in person: Your Grace.

Making an introduction: The Duke or Duchess of ….' whatever is the relevant place' e.g. The Duke of Kent.

Addressing a written communication: The Duke or Duchess of …. 'whatever is the relevant place'

Starting a written communication with: Dear Sir or Madam, or Dear Duke or Duchess of …. 'whatever is the relevant place'

Marquess and Marchioness

e.g. The Marquess of Bath

Addressing in person: Lord or Lady Bath

Making an introduction: Lord or Lady Bath

Addressing a written communication: The Marquess or Marchioness of Bath

Starting the communication with: Dear Lord or Lady Bath

Earl and Countess

Addressing in person: Lord or Lady Place

Making an introduction: Lord or Lady Place

Addressing a communication: The Earl or Countess of Place

Starting the communication: Dear Lord or Lady Place

Viscount & Viscountess

e.g. Viscount & Viscountess Linley

Addressing in person: Lord or Lady Linley

Making an introduction: Lord or Lady Linley

Addressing a communication: The Viscount or The Viscountess Linley

Starting the communication: Dear Lord or Lady Linley

Baron and Baroness

Addressing in person: Lord or Lady Place

Making an introduction: Lord or Lady Place

Addressing a communication: The Lord or The Lady Place

Starting the communication: Dear Lord or Lady Place

Sons and daughters of peers

The elder sons of Dukes, Marquesses, and Earls often hold courtesy titles (e.g.

The Earl of Place's eldest son would be styled Viscount Another place). Daughters and younger sons of Dukes, and Marquesses are usually styled The Lord or The Lady First-name and Family-name – as is the daughter or son of an Earl – who are addressed in person as Lord or Lady First-name.

The sons and daughters of Viscounts and Barons, and the younger sons of Earls, usually have the style 'The Honourable', frequently shortened to 'The Hon.', before their name. When introducing, however, you drop the Hon. unless the occasion is formal, in which case the Master of Ceremonies will announce the full name and title.

If a daughter with the title 'The Hon.' marries a non-titled person e.g. Mr John Smith, she would not be referred to as Mrs John Smith but as The Hon. Mrs Smith (meaning she retains her title before his surname).

A son styled The Hon. remains so regardless of whether or not he is married, however his wife would not be styled as The Hon. E.g., The Hon., and Mrs John Smith.

Baronet

Addressing in person: Sir John Smith (Wife – Lady Smith). Together would be Sir John & Lady Smith

Making an introduction: Sir John Smith (Wife – Lady Smith). Together would be Sir John & Lady Smith

Addressing a communication: Sir John Smith Bt (Wife – Lady Smith)

Starting the communication: Dear Sir John or Dear Lady Smith

Knight

Same as for a Baronet, but omit Bt., after the name in any communication.

Dames:

e.g. Dame Shirley Bassey:

Addressing in person: Dame Shirley

Making an introduction: Dame Shirley Bassey

Addressing a communication: Dame Shirley Bassey

Starting a communication: Dear Dame Shirley

Other titles and styles

There are numerous other titles and styles including the government and diplomatic service, Clergy, armed services, legal and medical professions etc. too numerous for the scope of this book.

However with a little research the necessary information can be found on the web.

Untitled people

Formal address for untitled men is Mr followed by the surname as Mr Smith, except on a written communication when the full name is used such as Mr John Smith or John Smith Esq.

NOTE: Mr & Esq. cannot be used at the same time.

Married women are addressed as Mrs followed by the surname as Mrs Smith except on a written communication when the full name is used such as Mrs John Smith.

Divorces

This can be confusing as the tendency today is for women to revert to their maiden names after a divorce, especially as many women conduct businesses and independent lives using their maiden names, and therefore there seems little point in changing.

The Correct form of address if a John & Mary Smith – (Mr & Mrs John Smith), get divorced, is normally as follows:

Mr John Smith's name remains the same however Mrs John Smith now uses her own Christian name and becomes Mrs Mary Smith retaining the title Mrs, indicating that she has been married.

If you are not certain how a person prefers to be addressed – ask!

A former wife of a hereditary peer is styled as though she were still married, except that her Christian name precedes her title, so, for example, the Duchess of Somewhere becomes:

Mary, Duchess of Somewhere. Note the ALL – IMPORTANT comma!

Widows

It is incorrect to use the woman's own first name rather than her late husband's (unless you are certain that is her preference) as this can imply the marriage ended prior to the death of her husband. So Mrs John Smith remains Mrs John Smith and not Mrs Mary Smith, which would indicate she was divorced.

The widow of a hereditary peer or a baronet usually has 'Dowager' before the title, so the Marchioness of Snooks becomes The Dowager Marchioness of Snooks, so Lady Snooks would become, The Dowager Lady Snooks. Occasionally the widow may prefer not to use Dowager and simply be styled Mary, Marchioness of Snooks

Partner/significant other/other half

(All titles which many find somewhat absurd!)

There is a great deal of confusion over couples who live together, unmarried, through choice, yet share their lives and are a definite couple.

The easiest solution is to treat them as if married, but address them each by their own name, inviting and referring to them together as a couple.

However with any communication I tend to leave off the prefix Miss – since the woman is known as part of a couple and therefore not strictly a Miss but neither is she a Mrs (unless of course, she is married to someone else, or a divorcee)

So, for example, I would write – Sir Benjamin Slade Bt and Kirsten Hughes or even Ms Kirsten Hughes.

index

Etiquette expert & Party guru Liz Brewer reveals the secrets of successful entertaining and etiquette in her second book on the subject.

Liz Brewer, party organiser to the stars, distills her 30 years of experience in her new book detailing each significant aspect of an event, with an assortment of ideas and advice for every existing or aspiring hostess.

Clearly illustrated, using her unique 'party tree' formula Liz Brewer covers every 'branch' of the party, from the initial idea to themes, decoration, entertainment, food, staff, and behaviour. The book fuses ideas with anecdotes from the author's own memorable events and experiences on the celebrity circuit.

Liz Brewer first shot to fame in the 60's when she swapped life as a debutante in favour of launching Portugal's first ever discotheque/nightclub.

The Club, 7 & 7 1/2 attracted an array of celebrities including Cliff Richards, The Shadows, Lulu, Cilla Black and Paul McCartney and gave its founder an appetite for extravagant events. Since then Liz has been featured in many television documentaries and shows including 5 x 6 part series for ITV's Ladette to Lady and as the UK's etiquette expert on Radio and TV.